THE ULTIMATE BOOK OF HOCKEY TRIVIA FOR KIDS

ERIC ZWEIG

Previously published as *Hockey Trivia for Kids, Hockey Trivia for Kids 2* and *Hockey Trivia for Kids 3.*

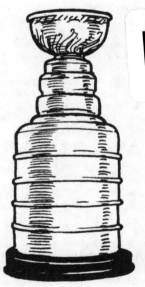

Illustrations by Bill Dickson
and Lorna Bennett

Scholastic Canada Ltd.

Toronto New York London Auckland Sydney
Mexico City New Delhi Hong Kong Buenos Aires

Scholastic Canada Ltd.
604 King Street West, Toronto, Ontario M5V 1E1, Canada

Scholastic Inc.
557 Broadway, New York, NY 10012, USA

Scholastic Australia Pty Limited
PO Box 579, Gosford, NSW 2250, Australia

Scholastic New Zealand Limited
Private Bag 94407, Botany, Manukau 2163, New Zealand

Scholastic Children's Books
Euston House, 24 Eversholt Street, London NW1 1DB, UK

www.scholastic.ca

Library and Archives Canada Cataloguing in Publication
Zweig, Eric, 1963-, author
The ultimate book of hockey trivia for kids / Eric Zweig ; Bill Dickson,
Lorna Bennett, illustrators.

Originally published in three separate volumes.
ISBN 978-1-4431-4609-8 (pbk.)

1. Hockey--Miscellanea--Juvenile literature. 2. National Hockey
League--Miscellanea--Juvenile literature. 3. Stanley Cup (Hockey)--
Miscellanea--Juvenile literature. I. Dickson, Bill, illustrator II. Bennett,
Lorna, 1960-, illustrator III. Zweig, Eric, 1963- . Hockey trivia for kids.
IV. Zweig, Eric, 1963- . Hockey trivia for kids 2. V. Zweig, Eric, 1963- .
Hockey trivia for kids 3. VI. Title.

GV847.25.Z943 2015   j796.962   C2015-901886-2

6 5 4 3 2   Printed in Canada 139   17 18 19 20 21

*To Amanda, a baseball fan; and to Néomi,
who seems to like hockey already.*
— Eric/Papa

Introduction

The Ultimate Book of Hockey Trivia for Kids. That's a lot
to live up to. When people think of trivia books, they
often think of questions and answers. There aren't really
many questions in this book, but I suppose there are
lots of answers . . . probably even some to questions you
haven't thought of.

In this book there are lots of stories about hockey's
past, but there are also plenty of stories about the stars
of the game today. After all, I've been a hockey fan for
a long time. I went to my first NHL game when I was
seven years old. I have to admit, I don't remember
knowing much about hockey before that night, but I've
learned an awful lot about it since then. In that game,
the Toronto Maple Leafs beat the California Golden Seals
3–1. The Seals (who played in Oakland) haven't existed
in the NHL for a very long time now. Maybe that has
something to do with why I enjoy telling stories about
the history of hockey!

I wasn't just a hockey fan as a boy. I was a pretty
good player too — but I was no Sidney Crosby. I've
said this before, and I think it's worth repeating: most
of us don't grow up to be NHL players or represent our
country at the Olympics. That doesn't mean we can't
have fun playing hockey. I think it's fun to read about
hockey too. I hope this book will be fun for you.

A Couple of Kids

Sidney Crosby was only 21 years old when the Pittsburgh Penguins won the Stanley Cup in 2009. He is the youngest person ever to captain his team to the championship. Jonathan Toews wasn't too much older when Chicago won the Cup in 2010. The Blackhawks' captain had celebrated his twenty-second birthday just a few weeks before he got to hoist the Stanley Cup.

Sidney Crosby at his first game as captain, October 5, 2007

The Great Debate

There's no denying it: hockey is Canada's game. We play it on ice. We play it on asphalt. We play it on tabletops and on video screens. There are more boys and girls registered to play minor hockey in Canada than there are anywhere else in the world. We've been playing it for a long time, and we're fiercely proud of it. But just where did it get its start?

Hockey has been around for hundreds of years. The first skates were made from bones or antlers that were tied with laces to the skater's footwear. Metal blades were eventually attached to the skater's boots with straps and buckles, or screwed right to the bottom of the boot. But exactly where hockey as we know it began is one of the most debated issues in sports.

The biggest debate is probably whether hockey got its start in Windsor, Nova Scotia, in the early 1800s, or Kingston, Ontario, in the mid-1800s. Early stories have soldiers playing on-ice versions of the games they had played at home in England, Scotland and Ireland which they called ice rugby, ice polo, ice hurley or ice hockey.

But one of the earliest mentions of the word "hockey" is from October 25, 1825. In a letter to a friend, explorer Sir John Franklin explains how he and his men skated and played a game they called hockey on a small lake in what is now Deline in the Northwest Territories.

A Brave New Game

The credit for making hockey so popular should go to
James Creighton. In 1872, Creighton, who had played
early games on ice while he was growing up in Halifax,
Nova Scotia, moved to Montreal. His new friends, who
already knew how to skate, were fascinated with this
Nova Scotia game. They asked Creighton to write down
a set of rules.

Creighton borrowed heavily from the game of rugby. Forward passing was not permitted. The ball had to be passed backwards or sideways. (Later, the top and bottom would be cut off the ball to keep it from bouncing over the boards around the rink. This was the first hockey puck.) There were nine players on each side, as well as one referee and two goal judges. The goal judges had to be especially brave — they stood right on the ice behind and between the goalposts. There wasn't a net or a crossbar, just two posts sticking up from the ice.

Then, on March 3, 1875, the *Montreal Gazette* reported that "a game of hockey" was to be played that evening at the Victoria Skating Rink. A new sport was born.

Today — more than 140 years later — the game you play on your local rink and the game played in packed NHL arenas is the direct descendant of the game once played by James Creighton and his friends in Montreal.

Captain Fantastic

Steve Yzerman was made captain of the Detroit Red Wings for the 1986–87 season. At the time, he was just 21 years old. That made him the youngest captain in Red Wings history. He went on to become the longest-serving captain in NHL history — wearing the "C" on his sweater for 20 years until he retired after the 2005–06 season.

Law of the Land

Is hockey really Canada's game? You bet. On May 12, 1994, a bill passed by the Canadian government became a law. Bill C-212 officially declared hockey as Canada's National Winter Sport.

The NHL is pretty particular about what goes on the ice. According to NHL rules, a hockey puck must be one inch (2.5 cm) thick with a three-inch (7.6 cm) diameter, and each puck must weigh between five-and-a-half and six oz. (156 and 170 g). And even though a puck is 90 percent rubber, it's actually made up of about a dozen different ingredients. Either coal dust or carbon black is used as filler, which also gives pucks their black colour. Other additives, such as sulphur, help strengthen it. Sher-Wood in Sherbrooke, Quebec, makes all NHL pucks.

Lord Stanley's Cup

Like hockey itself, the Stanley Cup is a lot older than the NHL. Teams have been competing for it since 1893.

Lord Frederick Arthur Stanley, the Earl of Preston, is the man behind the Stanley Cup. He was born in London, England, and served as the Governor General of Canada from 1888 to 1893. Lord Stanley was a fan of many sports, but he had never seen a hockey game until he came to Canada.

On February 4, 1889, Lord Stanley watched his first hockey game at the Montreal Winter Carnival. That game between the Montreal Victorias and the Montreal Amateur Athletic Association (AAA) was an exciting one, and the *Montreal Gazette* reported that Lord Stanley "expressed his great delight with the game of hockey and the expertise of the players." Soon after, three of his sons started playing for the Ottawa Rideau Rebels. Later, Lord Stanley's daughter Isobel became one of the first female hockey players in Canada.

On March 18, 1892, Lord Stanley announced that he was going to donate a championship trophy for hockey "considering the general interest which matches now elicit," which is just a fancy way of saying because it was very popular. He bought a silver cup just 18.5 cm (7.28 in.) high and appointed two trustees to take care of the silver trophy. The trophy was presented for the first time in 1893 to the Montreal Hockey Club, a team belonging to the Montreal AAA.

The original Stanley Cup

The shortest overtime period in NHL playoff history lasted only nine seconds. On May 18, 1986, Brian Skrudland of the Montreal Canadiens scored against Mike Vernon of the Calgary Flames to win 3–2.

Curses!

When the New York Rangers won the Stanley Cup
in 1940, it was the third time the team had won the
championship in just 14 seasons in the NHL. But their
next Stanley Cup victory wouldn't come until 1994 —
54 years later! Some fans believed the Rangers were
cursed.

Some stories said that Red Dutton had cursed the
Rangers. For many years, Dutton had run the New
York Americans. They were the first NHL team in
New York, but they never had the same success as the
Rangers. Dutton supposedly cursed the Rangers when
the Americans were forced to drop out of the NHL in
1942.

There is an even more famous story about how
the Rangers got cursed. During the 1940–41 season,
the bank loan to build the old Madison Square Garden
was finally paid off. The owners decided to burn their
mortgage papers inside the bowl of the Stanley Cup.
According to legend, this act angered the hockey gods
. . . and that's why it took the Rangers so long to win the
Cup again.

Early radio and TV broadcasts of NHL games always came on the air well after the game had started. This was because team owners were worried that people wouldn't buy tickets if they could listen to or watch the games for free. Hockey Night in Canada didn't show a whole game on TV until 1968–69 — its 16th season.

All-Star Honours

The idea of picking hockey's top players is almost as old as the game itself. As early as the 1890s, sportswriters published personal lists of All-Star players in their newspaper columns. The first big hockey All-Star Game was played on January 2, 1908. The game was held to raise money for the family of Hod Stuart, a top player who had drowned during the summer of 1907.

The NHL staged three All-Star Games during the 1930s. These games were all played to raise money for the families of players who had been killed or injured.

In 1946, a reporter from Chicago wanted to stage a game between the Stanley Cup champions and a team of NHL All-Stars. Money raised by the game would go toward local charities and a players' emergency fund. In 1947, the first official NHL All-Star Game was played in Toronto.

Except for two years in the 1950s, the early All-Star Games would match the Stanley Cup champions against the All-Stars. After 1968, the game usually matched All-Stars from one NHL conference against All-Stars from the other. In recent years, the players named as captains for the All-Star Game get to draft their own teams.

Gordie Howe is the oldest player to play in the All-Star Game at 51. Jeff Skinner is the youngest All-Star at age 18.

The Stanley Cup Story

The Stanley Cup is the oldest trophy competed for by professional athletes in North America. The "modern" sport of hockey was less than 20 years old when the first Stanley Cup champion was crowned in 1893.

Back in the 1890s, nobody was paid to play on a team. There also wasn't one big league that controlled the Cup like the NHL does today. Instead, the Cup was open to competition from the champions of any major provincial amateur association in Canada. That meant that instead of having a long playoff like there is today, the team that held the Stanley Cup had to face challenges from teams in other leagues . . . sort of like the way boxers and ultimate fighters face challenges for their title belts.

There were two men in charge of the Stanley Cup in the early days. These trustees, as they were called, had to decide which teams would be able to challenge the champions for the trophy. In 1906, the game — and the Stanley Cup — became professional. A new trophy (the Allan Cup) became the top prize for amateur teams. Even so, the Stanley Cup remained a challenge trophy a few years longer, only now it was available to the champions of any professional hockey league in Canada.

By 1914, there were only two professional leagues with teams good enough to compete for the Stanley Cup: The National Hockey Association (NHA) and the Pacific Coast Hockey Association (PCHA). Soon, the

PCHA added teams in the United States. The Stanley Cup was not just for Canadian teams anymore. In 1917, the National Hockey League (NHL) was formed and by 1926, it was the top league in hockey. Since 1927, only NHL teams have been allowed to compete for the Stanley Cup.

On January 3, 1931, Nels Stewart scored two goals four seconds apart in the third period (8:24 and 8:28) to lead the Montreal Maroons past the Boston Bruins 5–3. On December 15, 1995, Deron Quint tied Stewart's record for the two fastest goals in a game. He scored at 7:51 and 7:55 of the second period to lead the Winnipeg Jets past Edmonton 9–4.

What Happens in LEGOland . . .

In 2003, two replicas of the Stanley Cup were built out of 6,000 blocks of LEGO to promote a new line of LEGO NHL toys. One LEGO Stanley Cup went to NHL commissioner Gary Bettman. The other went on display at a sports show in Las Vegas . . . but then disappeared! There was a search for the missing LEGO Cup until a man from Arizona reported that he had bought it from someone for $50 while on a trip to Las Vegas. The man returned the LEGO Cup and was rewarded with Arizona Coyotes tickets and toys from LEGO's NHL line.

The real Stanley Cup with the LEGO Cup

Hall of Fame

It's something reserved for the greats of the game: induction into the Hockey Hall of Fame.

There's a special Selection Committee that decides which players are chosen for induction into the Hall. The rules state that a player must be retired for three years before he is eligible for induction. However, there have been some exceptions over the years.

Dit Clapper was the first to be inducted earlier than the three-year waiting period, in 1947. The next player to be so honoured was Maurice Richard in 1961. Known as "The Rocket," he was the NHL's all-time leader with 544 goals when he announced his retirement in September of 1960. The Hall of Fame building was set to open the following summer and inducting Richard was thought to be a fitting dedication.

Over the years, eight more players received this early honour "by reason of outstanding pre-eminence and skill": Ted Lindsay (1966), Red Kelly (1969), Terry Sawchuk (1971), Jean Beliveau (1972), Gordie Howe (1972), Bobby Orr (1979), Mario Lemieux (1997) and Wayne Gretzky (1999). After Gretzky was inducted, the Hall of Fame announced that it would no longer waive the three-year waiting period for anyone.

ON THE ROAD WITH STANLEY

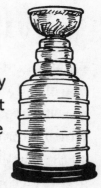

In 1993, the NHL marked the Stanley Cup's 100th birthday. They thought that letting each player on the winning team spend a whole day with the Cup would be a great way to celebrate. It turned out to be very popular with players and with fans. So, ever since 1995, the NHL has given all the players and the staff on the winning team their own special day to spend with the Stanley Cup that summer.

On February 8, 1975, Minnesota North Stars goalie Pete LoPresti recorded his first career shutout. That made him and Sam LoPresti the first father and son to both record shutouts in the NHL. Sam had played for Chicago back in the 1940s.

Will It Never End?

The longest game in NHL history was played on March 24, 1936, between the Detroit Red Wings and the Montreal Maroons. Detroit and Montreal were scoreless until the sixth overtime period! Finally, after 116:30 of extra play, Mud Bruneteau gave Detroit a 1–0 victory. Bruneteau scored his winning goal against Maroons goalie Lorne Chabot.

Phantom Joe

Hockey was a very different game when the NHL began. The only way to advance the puck was by skating with it and stickhandling. Forward passing was against the rules. The six men who started the game often played the full 60 minutes. Seasons were also much shorter, but since so few players got to play, the best ones scored plenty of goals.

Joe Malone was probably the best stickhandler in hockey when the NHL began. He was known as "Phantom Joe" because of his slick moves on the ice. It was as if he could disappear and reappear . . . like some kind of a ghost. On the first night in NHL history, Malone scored five goals for the Montreal Canadiens. He went on to lead the league with 44 goals during the 1917–18 season. He did it in just 20 games!

Malone's 44 goals remained an NHL record for 23 years. Today, the NHL record for goals in one season is 92. Still, no one has ever beaten Malone's scoring average of 2.2 goals per game. These days, a player would have to score 180 goals in 82 games to equal Malone's pace.

BY THE NUMBERS

Here is the complete list of Stanley Cup wins by current NHL teams:

NHL Team	Cup Wins
Montreal Canadiens	24*
Toronto Maple Leafs	13†
Detroit Red Wings	11
Boston Bruins	6
Chicago Blackhawks	6
Edmonton Oilers	5
New York Rangers	4
New York Islanders	4
Pittsburgh Penguins	3
New Jersey Devils	3
Philadelphia Flyers	2
Colorado Avalanche	2
Los Angeles Kings	2

Calgary Flames	1
Dallas Stars	1
Tampa Bay Lightning	1
Carolina Hurricanes	1
Anaheim Ducks	1

*Montreal's Stanley Cup wins include a victory in 1916, before the NHL was formed. †Toronto's Stanley Cup wins include victories by the Arenas in 1918 and the St. Pats in 1922, but not a victory by the Toronto Blueshirts in 1914, before the NHL was formed.

Octopus's Garden

There's an unusual tradition in Detroit that has been going on for more than 60 years: throwing an octopus onto the ice at Red Wings games, especially during the playoffs.

This strange tradition began back in 1952. At the time, there were only two rounds of playoffs in the NHL. That meant it took eight victories to win the Stanley Cup. Each tentacle of the octopus was symbolic of a

A linesman cleans up during a Detroit game.

win needed in the playoffs. Brothers Pete and Jerry Cusimano — who owned a local fish market — snuck a dead octopus into the Detroit Olympia arena for a playoff game on April 15, 1952. Pete tossed it onto the ice during the second period. The Red Wings beat the Canadiens that night to win the Stanley Cup with their eighth straight win in the playoffs. The octopus has been a good luck charm in Detroit ever since.

DID YOU KNOW?

According to David Keon, who works for the NHL public relations department in Toronto, 36 pucks are put into the freezer before a game at the Air Canada Centre. Usually it takes a dozen pucks to get through an average NHL game.

ON THE ROAD WITH STANLEY

Detroit Red Wings goalie Chris Osgood ate popcorn out of the Stanley Cup bowl while attending the world premiere of the Mike Myers film *The Love Guru* in 2008.

Mini Cups

Each player who wins the Stanley Cup receives a 33 cm (13 in.) miniature replica of the trophy. Each year, the mini Cups are engraved with the name of the team and all the players who won it that season, so it's a pretty special souvenir. The tradition of the mini Cups is thought to have begun informally in the early 1950s and became a regular event a few years later.

Buzzing About a Bruin

A researcher from the Boston area who helped discover a new species of wasp in Kenya named it after Bruins goalie Tuukka Rask. The wasp will be called *Thaumatodryinus tuukkaraski*. "That's pretty neat," said Rask, who obviously wasn't bugged by the idea.

When One Was Enough

When the Los Angeles Kings played the Minnesota North Stars on November 10, 1979, the puck they were using was never shot into the stands. They played the whole game with just one puck, which is on display at the Hockey Hall of Fame in Toronto.

DID YOU KNOW?

Arthur Farrell, who played for the Montreal Shamrocks, wrote the very first hockey book — way back in 1899. It's called **Hockey: Canada's Royal Winter Game.** *Only three copies are known to exist.*

Pucks in Space

Not only is hockey an international game, but it's had its adventures in space too. In October 1984, Dr. Marc Garneau, Canada's first astronaut, blasted into space aboard the shuttle *Challenger*. He carried a puck with him, which was later used in the ceremonial faceoff for the 1985 All-Star Game in Calgary. On January 22, 2013, astronaut Chris Hadfield — a huge Toronto Maple Leafs fan — took part in a ceremonial puck drop at the Air Canada Centre while he was on board the International Space Station. Of course, he needed a little help from some television special effects and a few former Maple Leafs stars here on Earth! Felix Potvin, Darcy Tucker and Darryl Sittler carried the puck from the roof of the arena down to centre ice.

Their Cups Runneth Over

The Montreal Canadiens have won the Stanley Cup more than any other team in hockey history — 24 times! The Canadiens' first Stanley Cup victory happened back in 1916, before the NHL was formed.

What's It Worth?

The original Stanley Cup bowl cost Lord Stanley 10 guineas at a silversmith's shop in London, England, in 1893. Ten guineas was worth a little bit more than $50 at the time. While that doesn't sound like a lot of money, the average Canadian worker in the 1890s wouldn't have been paid much more than about $50 a *month*!

As for the current trophy, it has an insurance value of $75,000. But, of course, the thrill of winning the Stanley Cup is priceless!

Outta This World

The Stanley Cup visited the Kennedy Space Center at Cape Canaveral, Florida, for a day in the summer of 2004 with Tampa Bay Lightning general manager Jay Feaster and the team's director of public relations, Jay Preble. The Cup visited *Discovery* as the shuttle prepared for its March 2005 launch and got a VIP tour of the orbiter (shuttle) as it was being prepared (but the Cup had to wait outside since it couldn't fit through the hatch). The Cup also toured the massive Vehicle Assembly Building and visited the launch pad. Later on, 600 NASA employees were able to see Stanley for themselves.

DID YOU KNOW?

Mike Sillinger holds the NHL record for the most teams played for. He suited up with 12 different clubs in his 17-year career.

A Puck by Any Other Name

Ever wonder why we call a puck a puck? Some think
it comes from Shakespeare's play *A Midsummer Night's
Dream*. In it, Puck, a mischievous sprite, appears and
disappears without warning — sort of like a hockey puck
in a crowd of sticks and skates.

More likely, though, the word comes from an Irish
game called hurling, which is a mixture of field hockey
and lacrosse. In Irish slang, the word "puck" is sometimes
used to mean smack or strike. For example, "a puck in the
puss" is like saying a punch in the mouth.

BY THE NUMBERS

Here is a history of NHL teams:

NHL Team	Franchise Date	First Season
Montreal Canadiens	November 26, 1917	1917–18
Toronto Maple Leafs[1]	November 26, 1917	1917–18
Boston Bruins	November 1, 1924	1924–25
New York Rangers	May 15, 1926	1926–27
Chicago Blackhawks	September 25, 1926	1926–27
Detroit Red Wings[2]	September 25, 1926	1926–27
Dallas Stars[3]	June 5, 1967	1967–68
Los Angeles Kings	June 5, 1967	1967–68
Philadelphia Flyers	June 5, 1967	1967–68
Pittsburgh Penguins	June 5, 1967	1967–68

NHL Team	Franchise Date	First Season
St. Louis Blues	June 5, 1967	1967–68
Buffalo Sabres	May 22, 1970	1970–71
Vancouver Canucks	May 22, 1970	1970–71
Calgary Flames[4]	June 6, 1972	1972–73
New York Islanders	June 6, 1972	1972–73
New Jersey Devils[5]	June 11, 1974	1974–75
Washington Capitals	June 11, 1974	1974–75
Colorado Avalanche[6]	June 22, 1979	1979–80
Edmonton Oilers	June 22, 1979	1979–80
Arizona Coyotes[7]	June 22, 1979	1979–80
Carolina Hurricanes[8]	June 22, 1979	1979–80
San Jose Sharks	May 9, 1990	1991–92
Ottawa Senators	December 16, 1991	1992–93

NHL Team	Franchise Date	First Season
Tampa Bay Lightning	December 16, 1991	1992–93
Florida Panthers	June 14, 1993	1993–94
Anaheim Ducks[9]	June 15, 1993	1993–94
Nashville Predators	June 25, 1997	1998–99
Winnipeg Jets[10]	June 25, 1997	1999–00
Columbus Blue Jackets	June 25, 1997	2000–01
Minnesota Wild	June 25, 1997	2000–01

[1] team name became Maple Leafs in February 1927
[2] team name became Red Wings in 1932–33
[3] transferred from Minnesota to Dallas on June 9, 1993
[4] transferred from Atlanta to Calgary on June 24, 1980
[5] transferred from Kansas City to Denver, then from Denver to New Jersey on June 30, 1982
[6] transferred from Quebec to Colorado on June 21, 1995
[7] transferred from Winnipeg to Phoenix on July 1, 1996
[8] transferred from Hartford to Carolina on June 25, 1997
[9] team known as Mighty Ducks of Anaheim until 2006–07
[10] transferred from Atlanta to Winnipeg on June 21, 2011

A Canadian Classic

The Canada Cup started in 1976, allowing the best NHL players to participate in a tournament against the top European teams. In 1996, the tournament was reorganized as the World Cup of Hockey.

For many fans, the 1987 Canada Cup was the greatest tournament ever. The Soviet Union had great players like Igor Larionov and Viacheslav Fetisov. Wayne Gretzky led Team Canada. "The Great One" had been the NHL's top scorer for eight straight seasons. Mario Lemieux had only been in the league for three years. He had done well, but being surrounded by so many stars on Team Canada seemed to make him even better.

To no one's surprise, Canada and the Soviets advanced to the three-game final in September 1987. Every game in the series was a thriller, with the lead going back and forth. The Soviets won the first game 6–5 in overtime. Two nights later, Canada won 6–5 in double overtime. Gretzky had five assists in the game. He set up Lemieux for three goals, including the winner. In the finale, Gretzky set up Lemieux again with 1:26 left in the game. Team Canada won — with a score of 6–5.

CUP CHRONICLES

Ever wonder why it says "Dominion Hockey Challenge Cup" on the Stanley Cup bowl? Lord Stanley didn't want to name the Cup after himself so he gave it that name. However, the trustees who were responsible for looking after the trophy decided right from the very beginning that the Cup should be named after the man who had donated it.

Super Mario

Bobby Orr called Mario Lemieux the most skilled player he had ever seen. Coming from Orr, it was high praise. But like Bobby Orr, Mario Lemieux's career was plagued by injuries, and even illness. Yet Lemieux was one of the greatest players in hockey history.

Lemieux was big, but he didn't throw his weight around. He beat players with speed and dekes. He led the NHL in scoring six times in his career. Only Wayne Gretzky has won more scoring titles.

Injuries forced Lemieux to retire in 1997. In 1999, he organized a group that bought the Pittsburgh Penguins. When he made a comeback in 2000, Lemieux became the first player in NHL history to play for a team that he also owned! He retired for good in 2006.

NAME GAME

The name Canadiens was chosen for Montreal's team to represent the French-speaking people of Quebec, who called themselves *canadiens*. Sometimes people refer to the Canadiens as the "Habs." According to stories, this nickname dates back to 1924. Tex Rickard, who owned Madison Square Garden in New York, was told that the "H" on the Canadiens sweater stood for *habitant*, a French word that was once used to describe the farmers of Quebec. Rickard was told that the French players on the team came from farms and that they were therefore "habitants" or "habs." Really, though, the "H" on the sweater stands for "hockey." The Montreal Canadiens' official name is le Club de Hockey Canadien.

The 1993 playoffs featured more overtime games than any season in NHL history. Of the 85 games played that spring, 28 went into overtime.

ON THE ROAD WITH STANLEY

Cornwall, Prince Edward Island, native Adam McQuaid of the Boston Bruins got to spend his day with the Stanley Cup in the summer of 2011. Prince Edward Island is famous for its potatoes, so he took the Cup to a local potato field and filled the bowl of the trophy with spuds.

The last non-NHL team to win the Stanley Cup was the Victoria Cougars, in 1925. The Cougars, who played in the Western Hockey League, beat the Montreal Canadiens.

Wicked-heiser

Hayley Wickenheiser is considered to be one of the best women's hockey players of all time. Wickenheiser first joined the Canadian National Women's Team in 1994 when she was just 15 years old. She has played hockey at the Winter Olympics in 1998, 2002, 2006, 2010 and 2014, winning four gold medals and one silver — and serving as Canada's flag-bearer for the 2014 opening ceremonies. Wickenheiser was also a member of the Canadian women's softball team at the 2000 Summer Olympics in Sydney, Australia, making her the first woman to represent Canada at both the Summer and Winter Olympic Games.

In 1998, Wickenheiser attended a training camp for Philadelphia Flyers rookies. In 2003, she joined a men's hockey team in Finland and scored her first goal for Kirkkonummi Salamat on January 11, 2003. That made her the first woman to score a goal in a men's professional hockey league.

Hayley Wickenheiser after her gold medal win in 2002

Since the introduction of the Stanley Cup in 1893, the name of the team that wins the prized mug has always been engraved right onto the trophy. The first team to engrave the names of all its players on the Stanley Cup was the Montreal Wanderers in 1907. Since 1924, every team that has won the Stanley Cup has engraved the names of its players on the trophy, as well as the names of owners, coaches, general managers and other members of the organization. The first woman to have her name engraved on the Stanley Cup was Marguerite Norris. She was the president of the Detroit Red Wings when they won the Cup in 1954 and 1955. In the years since then, the names of about a dozen women have been engraved on the Stanley Cup.

BY THE NUMBERS

Here's a look at the players who have won the Norris Trophy as the league's best defenceman the most times:

Player	Wins
Bobby Orr	8
Doug Harvey	7
Nicklas Lidstrom	7
Raymond Bourque	5
Chris Chelios	3
Paul Coffey	3
Denis Potvin	3
Pierre Pilote	3

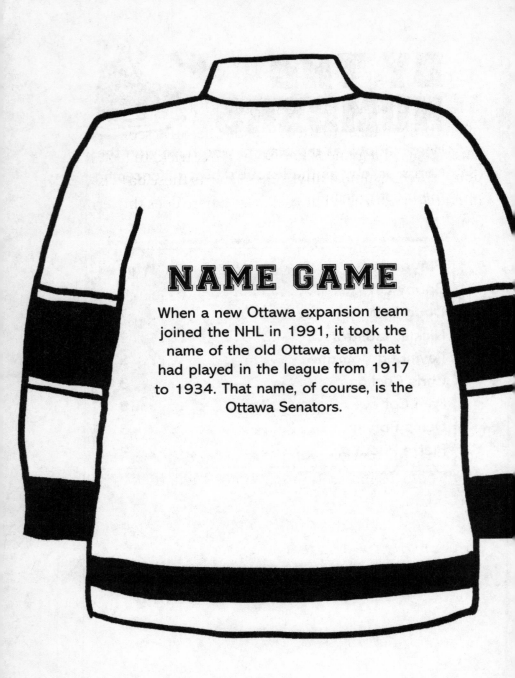

NAME GAME

When a new Ottawa expansion team joined the NHL in 1991, it took the name of the old Ottawa team that had played in the league from 1917 to 1934. That name, of course, is the Ottawa Senators.

Hat Trick

When a player scores three goals in a game, fans will often throw hats onto the ice. That's because scoring three goals in a game is known as a hat trick. In fact, doing three of almost anything in sports these days is often referred to as a hat trick. But where does the term come from?

Hat trick actually comes from the English game of cricket. It refers to a bowler who takes three wickets with three straight balls. (A bowler is like the pitcher in baseball. Taking three straight wickets is like striking out three straight batters. In cricket, this is very rare.)

Apparently, back in the 1800s, it was the custom that if a bowler could take three straight wickets in three successive balls, his team would buy him a new hat. Some people tell the story a bit differently though. They say that if the bowler achieved this impressive feat, he would pass his hat around the stands and fans would fill it with money.

It's often said that Sammy Taft brought the term to hockey in the 1940s. Taft lived in Toronto and sold hats from a store on Spadina Avenue. When a player scored three goals in a game at Maple Leaf Gardens, he would give the player a free hat.

Taft certainly did a lot to make it a popular term, but the truth is people had been referring to three goals as a hat trick in hockey since at least the 1920s. On December 26, 1930, legendary sportswriter Michael J. Rodden wrote this in his column about a New York

Rangers game: "Bunny Cook had a field day, getting three consecutive goals to perform the hat trick deluxe."

Not So Original Six

When people talk about the old days of the NHL, they often talk about the "Original Six." That's because for many years there were only six teams in the league. The Original Six are: the Montreal Canadiens, Toronto Maple Leafs, Boston Bruins, New York Rangers, Chicago Blackhawks and Detroit Red Wings.

Really, though, most of the Original Six teams aren't original at all!

When the NHL was formed in 1917, it actually had five teams: the Montreal Canadiens, Montreal Wanderers, Toronto Arenas, Ottawa Senators and Quebec Bulldogs. The Quebec team didn't have enough money to start right away, and the Wanderers had to drop out of the league early because their arena burned down. So, in a way, Montreal, Toronto and Ottawa were the NHL's Original Three.

By the end of the 1920s, the NHL had grown from three teams to ten. In addition to Toronto, Montreal and Ottawa, there were now seven others: the Montreal Maroons, Boston Bruins, Detroit Cougars, Chicago Black

Hawks, New York Rangers, New York Americans and Pittsburgh Pirates.

Then the 1930s came along. Times were tough because of the Great Depression, and many teams were losing money. The NHL began to lose some of its teams. The teams from both Pittsburgh and Ottawa had to move. Pittsburgh became the Philadelphia Quakers. Ottawa became the St. Louis Eagles. Still, the teams lost money and soon both went out of business, followed by the Montreal Maroons and the New York Americans. By 1942, the NHL was left with just six teams: the so-called Original Six. They remained the only teams in the league until 1967.

Uphill Battle

Al Hill holds the record for most points by a player in his first NHL game. Hill was called up to the Philadelphia Flyers on February 14, 1977. He had five points that night: two goals and three assists. He played only eight more games for the Flyers that year and added only one more assist.

Chris Chelios is the oldest player ever to win the Stanley Cup. He won it at age 46 in 2008 with the Detroit Red Wings.

The Finnish Flash

Nobody in NHL history has burst onto the scene like Teemu Selanne. In his first season of 1992–93, Selanne set a rookie record for goals that may never be matched.

The Winnipeg Jets selected Selanne 10th overall at the 1988 NHL Draft. It took him four years to leave his home in Finland, but it was well worth the wait. In his first game in 1992, Selanne picked up his first assist. His first goal came two nights later . . . and Selanne just kept on scoring. Mike Bossy had held the NHL rookie record for goals with 53 — Selanne scored his 54th with more than a month left in the season. At the end of the season, Selanne had 76 goals. Only three players in NHL history had ever scored more. Selanne finished with 132 points, setting another rookie record.

Though he never matched the huge numbers of his first season, Selanne continued to be a dangerous offensive player. When he scored 48 goals for the Anaheim Ducks in 2006–07, it was the seventh time in his career that he'd scored 40 or more. At the age of 36, Selanne was the oldest player in NHL history to score more than 45 goals in a single season.

Overtime Over Time

The rules for overtime in the regular season have changed a lot during the history of the NHL. When the league began in the 1917–18 season, any game that was tied after 60 minutes would continue into overtime for however long it took until a team finally won . . . just like in the playoffs. That remained the rule until the end of the 1920–21 season.

Beginning in 1921–22, the NHL limited overtime to just one 20-minute period. This was the rule until the end of the 1926–27 season. In 1927–28, the NHL decided the overtime period should only be 10 minutes long. If no one had scored by the end of the set overtime period, the game would end in a tie.

During the seasons from 1917–18 to 1927–28, overtime was always sudden death. That meant whichever team scored first was the winner. Starting in 1928–29, overtime was played for a full 10 minutes no matter how many goals were scored! If both teams scored, the game ended in a tie. When overtime returned to the regular season in 1983, it became a five-minute, sudden-death period. Then, in the 2005–06 season, the league decided that games would go to shootouts to decide a winner if no one scored in overtime.

Flower Power

Guy Lafleur's speed and skill made him the most exciting player in the NHL during the 1970s. Lafleur led the NHL in points three years in a row, from 1975–76 to 1977–78, and topped 50 goals for six straight seasons. He won the Hart Trophy as MVP twice and helped the Canadiens win the Stanley Cup five times.

Lafleur was known as "The Flower," the English translation of his last name. French fans called him "le Demon Blond" (The Blond Demon) because of his blazing speed and long blond hair.

But by the 1980s, Lafleur was slowing down. After 19 games of the 1984–85 season, he had scored just two goals. He decided to retire on November 26, 1984. But around the time he was elected to the Hockey Hall of Fame in 1988, Lafleur announced he was going to make a comeback. He signed with the New York Rangers, and then spent two seasons with the Quebec Nordiques before retiring for good in 1991.

ON THE ROAD WITH STANLEY

On August 7, 2009, Sidney Crosby turned 22 and celebrated with the Stanley Cup and the men and women of Canada's military. Crosby's Pittsburgh Penguins had won the Cup a few weeks earlier, and on the morning of his birthday, it arrived at the Halifax airport. A Sea King helicopter from the Canadian Armed Forces carried Crosby, his father and the Stanley Cup down to the Halifax dockyard. They landed on the deck of the HMCS *Preserver*, a ship from the Canadian navy. After a reception with military personnel and their families, a light armoured vehicle took Crosby and the Cup through the city to the old fortress known as the Halifax Citadel. Later, back in his hometown of Cole Harbour, just outside of Halifax, *goalie* Sidney Crosby led his team to a Stanley Cup victory in a game of roller hockey with his childhood friends.

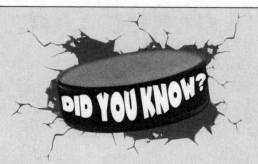

The original base of the Stanley Cup had a small silver band around it where the names of the winning teams could be engraved. Adding the name of the winning team each year would eventually cause the Stanley Cup to grow.

Locked Out

As the NHL expanded during the 1990s, so too did players' salaries. Then, due to disagreements about how much money the players should be paid, in 2004–05 the NHL became the first major professional sports league to cancel a whole season. Money wasn't the only issue, but it was the most important one. The NHL owners wanted players' salaries to be linked to the money that the league made. That meant players would only earn a certain percentage of the money the league made. The players called it a "salary cap," and they didn't want one.

Because of the disagreement between the players and owners, a lockout began at midnight on September 15, 2004. That meant no games would be played until the players and owners reached an agreement. Many people feared the lockout might last longer than one season. (The NHL had a previous lockout back in 1994–95, and later suffered through another one in 2012–13, but neither of those wiped out an entire season, let alone more than one season.) Fortunately on July 13, 2005, a new, six-year agreement was reached.

The new NHL season began on October 5, 2005, with 15 games on the schedule. That meant it was the first time that all 30 teams had played on the same night.

The biggest crowd anywhere in the NHL that night was in Tampa Bay. The arena there is only supposed to hold 19,758 people, but the crowd reached 22,120. The Lightning had won the Stanley Cup in 2004, but because of the lockout, fans in Tampa Bay had been forced to wait more than a year to watch their team raise the championship banner.

Can I Help You?

Wayne Gretzky retired as an NHL player in 1999. At that time, he held or shared 61 different NHL records. Even though he still holds the NHL records for most goals in a season and most goals in a career, Gretzky never really considered himself to be a great scorer — really! He was most proud of his skill as a playmaker: he liked to help his teammates score. In his career, Gretzky had 1,963 assists. That's more than anyone else in NHL history. Not only that, it means Gretzky has more assists than any other player has total points!

Cup or Kids?

In the fall of 2010, the city of Cornwall, Ontario, honoured hometown hero Newsy Lalonde. Lalonde had been one of the greatest players in hockey in the early 1900s. He starred with the Montreal Canadiens and led them to their first Stanley Cup victory in 1916. Henri Richard, another Canadiens superstar, was on hand for the festivities. During a quiet moment, somebody asked Richard how many grandchildren he had. He proudly answered eleven, and began counting off the names on his fingers. Twice he got to ten, and then had to stop. "I'm sorry," he finally said. "It's ten grandchildren, not eleven. I keep getting that confused with Stanley Cups!" Richard had won the Stanley Cup a record 11 times in his career.

On March 1, 1919, Newsy Lalonde became the first player to score five goals in an NHL playoff game. Over the years, Maurice Richard, Darryl Sittler, Reggie Leach and Mario Lemieux have all tied Newsy's record, but no one has ever broken it.

How Tall Is the Cup?

The original Stanley Cup bowl stood 18.5 cm (7.28 in.) tall and measured 29 cm (11 in.) across the top. (The bowl on top of the trophy today is the exact same size.) When it was mounted on its original base, the entire trophy was just under 29 cm (11 in.) tall as well.

Today, the Stanley Cup stands nearly a metre (3 ft.) tall. It weighs 15.5 kg (34.5 lb.). That's pretty heavy . . . but not so heavy that winning players can't pick it up and parade it around!

ON THE ROAD WITH STANLEY

Brad Stuart of the Detroit Red Wings had a special Stanley Cup–shaped cake baked for his day with the Cup in the summer of 2008. Stuart's 13-year-old stepdaughter insisted on eating her piece of cake right out of the Stanley Cup bowl.

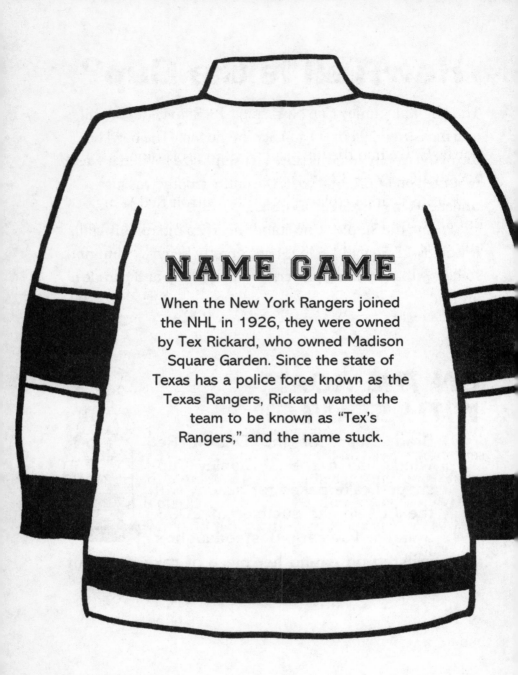

NAME GAME

When the New York Rangers joined the NHL in 1926, they were owned by Tex Rickard, who owned Madison Square Garden. Since the state of Texas has a police force known as the Texas Rangers, Rickard wanted the team to be known as "Tex's Rangers," and the name stuck.

Red Wings, Grey Hair

Gordie Howe had the longest career in professional hockey history — 32 years!

For 25 years, he played with the Detroit Red Wings. But after the 1970–71 season, he retired. He must have missed it pretty badly, because two years later, he once again took to the ice. A new league, the World Hockey Association (WHA), had formed, and the Houston Aeros signed Gordie's sons, Mark and Marty. Even though Gordie was 45 years old, he decided to join his sons on the ice.

Gordie and his sons played six seasons together in the new league. Then, in 1979–80, four teams from the WHA joined the NHL. Gordie was 51 years old. That season he played all 80 games, and scored 15 goals, in what would end up being his final season in the NHL.

Over the years, only Chris Chelios has equalled Gordie Howe's 26 seasons in the NHL, and though a few players have come close, no one has matched his 1,767 games. Only Wayne Gretzky has more than his 801 NHL goals. And when his WHA totals are included, Gordie played for 32 years and in 2,186 games, scoring 975 goals. Not bad for a grandfather.

Cougar Cubs

According to stories, after Lester Patrick's Victoria Cougars won the Stanley Cup in 1925, Lester's sons Lynn and Muzz found the trophy in their basement and decided to scratch their names on it with a nail. Their names would be properly engraved on the Stanley Cup 15 years later as NHL stars with the 1940 New York Rangers.

The original Stanley Cup bowl is on display at the Hockey Hall of Fame in Toronto.

Silver and Gold

Eight players in hockey history have won the Stanley Cup and an Olympic gold medal in the same season. The first was Ken Morrow in 1980 when he won Olympic gold for the United States and the Stanley Cup with the New York Islanders. In 2002, Brendan Shanahan and Steve Yzerman won gold for Canada and the Stanley Cup with Detroit. In 2010, Duncan Keith, Brent Seabrook and Jonathan Toews won gold for Canada and the Stanley Cup with Chicago. In 2014, Drew Doughty and Jeff Carter won gold for Canada and the Stanley Cup with Los Angeles.

Silver and Gold and Then Some

In addition to his Olympic gold medal in 2010, Jonathan Toews was also named the tournament's best forward and was selected to the All-Star Team. Then, in addition to winning the Stanley Cup, he won the Conn Smythe Trophy as playoff MVP. Not a bad season!

Wandering Around

The Montreal Wanderers won the Stanley Cup in 1906, 1907, 1908 and 1910, but they weren't always the best keepers of the Cup.

According to old stories, the Wanderers once forgot all about the coveted trophy. They left it at a photographer's studio after having their team picture taken in 1907. A woman working in the studio found it and thought the Cup would make a lovely flowerpot. She used it to hold flowers for several months before someone from the Wanderers finally came back to claim it!

Right on the Mark

Mark Messier became a star with the Edmonton Oilers in the 1980s. He became a legend with the New York Rangers in 1994.

Messier won the Stanley Cup four times with the Oilers in the 1980s. After Wayne Gretzky was traded in 1988, Messier led the team to another championship in 1990. The Rangers hoped he could do the same thing for them when they signed him in 1991.

The Rangers finished the 1993–94 season in first place. They knocked off the Islanders and the Capitals in the first two rounds of the playoffs, but ran into trouble against the Devils in the Eastern Conference Finals. New Jersey was up 3–2 in the series, heading into Game 6. Messier promised the media that the Rangers would win . . . and made good on his promise. He scored three goals in the third period for a 4–2 win. They wrapped up the series with Stephane Matteau's double overtime winner in the seventh game.

The Rangers faced the Canucks in the Stanley Cup Finals. They jumped out to a 3–1 lead in the series, but almost let it slip away. When they won 3–2 in Game 7, it was Mark Messier who scored the winning goal.

NAME GAME

When Detroit entered the NHL in 1926, the team was known as the Cougars. That's because the franchise had previously been known as the Victoria Cougars. But in 1930, the name was changed to the Detroit Falcons. Since their sweaters were red and white, in 1932, team president James Norris changed the name to the Red Wings. Norris had grown up in Montreal where he had been a member of the Montreal Amateur Athletic Association, whose sports teams were known as the "Winged Wheelers." Since Detroit is known as the Motor City (because so many cars are built there), Norris thought that their winged wheel logo would be a perfect fit and put a wheel with a wing on their sweaters.

Pick That Up

In 1950, Ted Lindsay picked up the Stanley Cup and skated around with it after the Detroit Red Wings' victory over the New York Rangers. Since then, players skating around the ice with the Cup has become a beloved hockey tradition. Lindsay may not have been the very first to do this though. Old newspaper stories say that Lou Trudel skated around with the Cup after the Chicago Black Hawks won it way back in 1934.

Growing Pains

In 1902, the first ring on the original Stanley Cup became filled with the list of winning teams. For the next few years, teams engraved their names onto the bowl itself. A couple of teams even engraved their names right inside the bowl. But finally, in 1909, a bigger base was added to the bottom, with a second silver ring for more names.

Money Matters

Today's NHL players can make millions of dollars per season. However, players stop getting a regular paycheque once the playoffs start. Often you'll hear people saying things like "the players are only playing for pride" when they're going after the Stanley Cup. That's not entirely true. According to the NHL's Collective Bargaining Agreement, a total of $13 million is put aside for the players on teams that make the playoffs. The further their team goes, the more of that money they earn. The team that wins the Stanley Cup gets a total payment of $3.75 million in bonus money to be split among its players.

On January 2, 1980, Gordie Howe became the first player in NHL history to play in five different decades. Howe had made his NHL debut on October 16, 1946, with the Detroit Red Wings.

Mr. Goalie

Glenn Hall, known as "Mr. Goalie," was one of the greatest netminders in NHL history.

Hall was signed by the Detroit Red Wings in 1949, but didn't become their starting goalie until the 1955–56 season. He played every minute of all 70 games for Detroit that year and led the NHL with 12 shutouts. Hall played every minute of every game for Detroit again in 1956–57.

In the summer of 1957, Hall was traded to Chicago. He continued to play every minute of every game for the Black Hawks for the next four seasons. In 1961, Hall helped Chicago win the Stanley Cup. It was the first time they had won it since 1938.

On November 7, 1962, Hall finally took a seat on the bench. He had pinched a nerve in his back during practice, and it became too painful for him to play. Hall had started the game, but took himself out after Boston scored midway through the first period. Until then, Hall had played 502 games in a row during the regular season without missing a single minute. He had also played in 49 straight playoff games.

Boucher Blanks Them

For most of his NHL career, Brian Boucher was a backup goalie. Yet for a brief stretch with the Phoenix Coyotes during the 2003–04 season, Boucher was better than almost anyone in NHL history. Between December 31 and January 9, Boucher shut out his opponents five games in a row.

The streak began with a 4–0 win over the Los Angeles Kings. After his third consecutive shutout, the hockey world began to take notice. The modern record for shutouts in a row was four, set by Canadiens goalie Bill Durnan in 1948–49. Durnan had won the Vezina Trophy as the NHL's best goalie six times in his seven-year career. Could someone like Brian Boucher really break his record?

On January 7, 2004, Boucher tied the record with a 3–0 win in Washington. Two days later, he broke it with a 2–0 win in Minnesota. On January 11, Boucher almost made it six in a row. He allowed just one goal in a 1–1 tie with Atlanta. The goal came early in the first period and went in because of a lucky bounce off Coyotes defenceman David Tanabe.

DID YOU KNOW?

In 1944–45 Montreal Canadiens legend Maurice "Rocket" Richard was the first player in NHL history to score 50 goals in a single season. Richard was also the first player in NHL history to score 500 goals in his career. He accomplished that feat on October 19, 1957. Both marks remain important milestones in the career of any great NHL scorer.

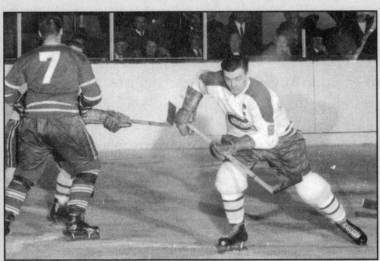

Maurice Richard eyes the goal.

Saint Patrick

As an NHL rookie in 1985–86, Patrick Roy seemed to be a bundle of nerves. His head was constantly bobbing up and down as he craned his neck from side to side. Roy even admitted that he sometimes liked to talk to his goalposts!

Roy may have looked strange, but he was good — especially in the playoffs. Montreal wasn't expected to go very far that year, but Roy led the Canadiens all the way to the Stanley Cup. And in 1993, his performance was even more amazing.

After losing the opening game of the 1993 playoffs in overtime, Roy promised his teammates that he wouldn't surrender another overtime goal that year. And he didn't. The Canadiens played 10 more overtime games that spring and won them all. Until then, no NHL team had ever won more than six overtime games. Three of Roy's victories came in the Finals, where the Canadiens defeated the Los Angeles Kings to win the Stanley Cup once again.

"When Patrick makes a promise, he keeps it," said teammate Mike Keane. "He said he was going to shut the door, and he did."

ON THE ROAD WITH STANLEY

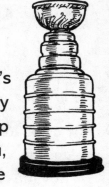

It's hard to beat the day Detroit's Chris Chelios spent with the Stanley Cup in 2008. Chelios had the Cup at his summer home in Malibu, California, and took it to a couple of celebrity beach parties. Among those who spent time with the Cup that day were musician Kid Rock, TV star Jeremy Piven, and movie star Cuba Gooding Jr. When word began to spread about the party with the Stanley Cup, Tom Hanks and Sylvester Stallone both dropped by to check it out.

CUP CHRONICLES

In 1895, a team from Queen's University in Kingston, Ontario, became the first team to challenge the champions for the Stanley Cup. Queen's got to play a one-game challenge against the Montreal AAA, but they lost 5–1. Queen's also challenged for the Cup in 1899 and 1906, but lost those times too.

On December 24, 1972, the Los Angeles Kings beat the Oakland Seals 5–3 in the last NHL game ever played on Christmas Eve. Serge Bernier scored four goals for Los Angeles. Earlier that evening, Chicago beat Toronto 5–1 and the Rangers beat Detroit 5–0. Since 1973, the NHL has always had a break in the schedule for Christmas Eve and Christmas Day.

Differently Abled

One of the most popular Paralympic sports is an adaptation of traditional ice hockey. Sledge hockey was invented in 1961 by three wheelchair athletes on a frozen lake in Stockholm, Sweden. It's played on specially designed sleds that have skate blades under the seats. Players sit on the sleds, holding a stick in each hand, and use their sticks to pass, shoot and stickhandle the puck, as well to manoeuvre their sleds. The game's rules are basically the same as hockey's, and today it's popular wherever hockey is played.

From Sweden, sledge hockey spread quickly to neighbouring Norway, and then to England. After a few false starts in Canada, the game got going for real in Alberta in 1980. It had spread across the country by 1983. The Canadian team won the gold medal at the first World Cup of sledge hockey in 1991, marking the first time in 25 years that Sweden had lost a game! Sledge hockey entered the Paralympic Winter Games in 1994, and the first World Championship tournament was held in 1996.

The Last Goal He Ever Scored

Toronto hockey fans loved Bill Barilko. He was a solid defenceman who was as handsome as he was hard-hitting. In five seasons with the Maple Leafs, from 1946–47 to 1950–51, he helped Toronto win the Stanley Cup four times. The Cup Final in 1951 was one of the most thrilling in hockey history. Each of the five games played by Toronto and the Montreal Canadiens went into overtime.

Leafs coach Joe Primeau had told Barilko to concentrate on defence. He didn't want him jumping into the offensive zone. Yet at 2:53 of overtime in Game 5, Barilko raced in from the Montreal blueline. He dove at the puck and chopped it toward the net. Barilko's shot went in, and the Leafs won the Stanley Cup! Sadly, it was the last goal he ever scored.

Bill Barilko disappeared that summer. He was on a fishing trip when his plane crashed in the woods of northern Ontario. The Maple Leafs didn't win the Stanley Cup again until 1962. By strange coincidence, that was the same year that Barilko's remains were finally discovered.

More Growing Pains

In 1924, the Montreal Canadiens added a band to the Stanley Cup and not only filled it with the names of their players, but also their coaches and management staff. From that year on, every team that has won the Stanley Cup has also engraved the names of coaches and management. Between 1924 and 1947, a brand new band had to be added to the Stanley Cup nearly every year. By 1947, the Cup stood at its current height but most of it measured only a few centimetres across. People often refer to the Stanley Cup of this era as the "elephant leg" Cup, the "cigar" Cup or the "stove pipe" Cup.

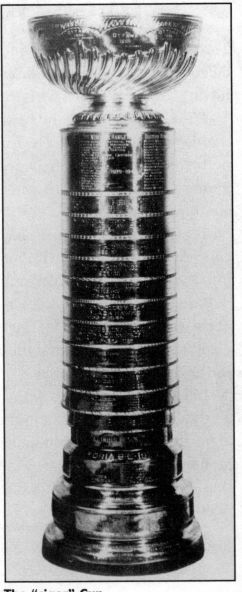

The "cigar" Cup

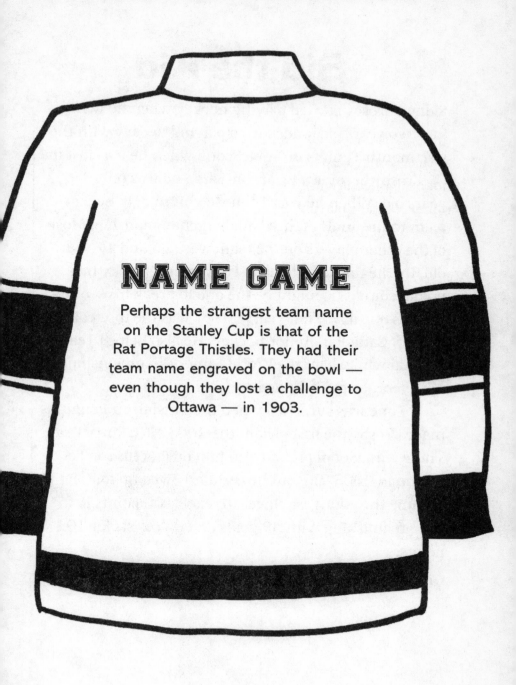

NAME GAME

Perhaps the strangest team name on the Stanley Cup is that of the Rat Portage Thistles. They had their team name engraved on the bowl — even though they lost a challenge to Ottawa — in 1903.

Sid the Kid

Sidney Crosby started playing hockey when he was just two years old, and started playing hockey with the Dartmouth Timbits in Nova Scotia when he was just five.

Crosby became a local star when he was only 10 years old. When he was 14, he led his midget hockey team to the finals of the Canadian championship. Most of the other players on the team were 16 and 17 years old. By the time Crosby was 16, Wayne Gretzky had predicted that he might be the one to break his scoring records one day. That year, Crosby was the top scorer in all of Canadian junior hockey. He also helped Team Canada win gold at the World Junior Championship. The next year, he did it all again.

No one was surprised when the Pittsburgh Penguins made Crosby the first pick in the 2005 NHL Entry Draft. There was a lot of pressure on him during his rookie season in 2005–06, but he certainly lived up to it: he became the youngest player to reach 100 points in a season, finishing with 39 goals and 63 assists for 102 points.

Scoring Is an Art

The NHL's scoring leader — the player who gets the most points, which includes goals and assists — is awarded the Art Ross Trophy. Strangely, Art Ross himself only had one point in his entire NHL career. Of course, he only played three games! Ross was a star defenceman who played most of his career before the NHL was formed. Later, he became the first coach and general manager of the Boston Bruins.

Ross planned to donate a trophy to the NHL in 1941. He wanted his trophy to go to the NHL's most outstanding player. But the NHL already had the Hart Trophy, which goes to the Most Valuable Player during the regular NHL season. Instead, it was decided that Ross's trophy would be used to reward the NHL's scoring leader. It was first presented to Elmer Lach in 1948.

DID YOU KNOW?

On May 4, 2009, Alex Ovechkin and Sidney Crosby both scored their first career playoff hat tricks in the same game. Ovechkin's Capitals beat Crosby's Penguins 4–3.

Boom Boom and Bobby

Hockey's second 50-goals-in-a-season scorer after Maurice Richard was also a member of the Montreal Canadiens. Bernie "Boom Boom" Geoffrion reached the milestone in 1960–61. His nickname was "Boom Boom" because when he took a shot — boom! It was powerful.

But Bobby Hull also had a powerful shot. Hull played for the Chicago Black Hawks, and one year after Geoffrion scored his 50 goals, Hull made it to 50 too — on the final night of the 1961–62 season.

Four years later, Hull scored his 50th goal of the season after Chicago had played just 57 games. That meant Hull had 13 more games to become the first player in NHL history to score more than 50 goals in one season. It seemed like a cinch. But it wasn't.

Over the next five days, Hull couldn't score a single goal. Not only that, no one on the Black Hawks could score. Chicago was shut out for three straight games! Finally, on March 12, 1966, Hull blasted a shot past Cesar Maniago of the New York Rangers. The new goal-scoring record was his. He scored three more times before the year was over, and ended the 1965–66 season with 54 goals. Hull also won the Art Ross Trophy that year. His 54 goals plus 43 assists gave him 97 points, which also set an NHL record.

Manon Rheaume was a goalie who helped the Canadian National Women's Team win the World Championship in 1992. That year she also became the first woman to play major junior hockey in Canada. She played one game for Trois-Rivières in the Quebec Major Junior Hockey League. Then, on September 23, 1992, Manon Rheaume became the first woman to play in the NHL. She played for the Tampa Bay Lightning in a pre-season game against the St. Louis Blues.

Rinks Rule

The very first rule in the NHL rulebook is about the ice and is called quite simply "Rink." Here's what it says: "The game of 'Ice Hockey' shall be played on an ice surface known as the 'RINK.'"

No rink dimensions were included as part of the NHL Official Rules until 1929–30. That season, they were officially made 200 ft. (61 m) by 85 ft. (26 m). This was the size of the ice surface at the Victoria Skating Rink in Montreal where the first game of modern hockey was played on March 3, 1875. These dimensions are still used today.

Guy's Got It

In the years before everyone on the winning team was allowed to spend a day with the Stanley Cup, players didn't get to see the trophy much. In the early days, the Stanley Cup would often go on display in a store window for a few days somewhere in the city that won it. Even in more recent times, there would usually be a couple of team parties that the Stanley Cup got taken to, but mostly it was kept out of sight. Often, when stories come up about something crazy that happened to the Stanley Cup, it's hard to prove if they're true or not.

One of those famous stories is about Guy Lafleur of the Montreal Canadiens, who "borrowed" the Stanley Cup for a day in 1978.

After the Canadiens held their Stanley Cup victory parade, a Montreal club official locked the Cup in the trunk of his car for safekeeping. Somehow, Lafleur got it out and made off with it. The next morning, he called his father in his hometown of Thurso, Quebec, and told him to look on his front lawn. There on the grass, glistening in the morning sun, was the Stanley Cup!

After the Stanley Cup's adventure with Guy Lafleur, players on the winning team started to get a little more private time to spend with the trophy before they were given their own official day years later.

Stickin' It to Him

The Los Angeles Kings had won Game 1 of the 1993 Stanley Cup Finals against the Montreal Canadiens and were leading 2–1 in Game 2 late in the third period. Canadiens trainer Gerard Lefebvre had told coach Jacques Demers that Los Angeles defenceman Marty McSorley was using an illegal stick. Demers decided to call for a measurement. If Lefebvre was wrong, Montreal would get a delay-of-game penalty. It turned out that he was right, though, and McSorley was the one who got sent to the penalty box. Montreal scored the tying goal on the power play and then won the game in overtime. The Canadiens didn't lose again in the series, taking the Stanley Cup in five games.

CUP CAPERS

Bobby Hull joined the Chicago Black Hawks for the 1957–58 season. At the time, Chicago was the worst team in the NHL. The league only had six teams, and Chicago had finished sixth 9 times in the last 11 years. They missed the playoffs 11 times in 12 years. But, with players like Bobby Hull, Stan Mikita and Glenn Hall, the Black Hawks improved quickly. In 1961, they finally won the Stanley Cup — for the first time since 1938.

Chicago's Stanley Cup victory ended a streak of five championships by the Montreal Canadiens. In fact, Chicago had beaten the Canadiens in the semifinals before winning the Stanley Cup in a series against Detroit. Then, in 1962, Chicago and Montreal met in the semifinals for a second straight year. The Black Hawks won again.

During the 1962 semifinals, the Stanley Cup was on display in the lobby of the Chicago Stadium. A Canadiens fan broke into the display case and tried to steal it, but was quickly caught. His excuse? He couldn't stand a second straight season without seeing the Stanley Cup in Montreal.

Stolen Silverware

A Toronto policeman named Harold "Lumpy" Lambert made one of the biggest saves in hockey history back in 1969. Thieves had stolen three of the NHL's trophies from the Hockey Hall of Fame: the Hart, Conn Smythe and Calder. After tough detective work, Lambert found them wrapped in green garbage bags near a prison outside Toronto.

Art Ross was the first coach in NHL history to pull his goalie for an extra attacker. Ross did it on March 26, 1931, during a semifinal playoff series. His Boston Bruins lost the game 1–0 to the Montreal Canadiens.

You Gotta Have Hart

The Hart Trophy, which honours the player who is "adjudged to be the most valuable to his team," is the NHL's oldest individual award. Dr. David Hart donated it in 1923. His son Cecil Hart was an executive with the Montreal Canadiens. Frank Nighbor of the Ottawa Senators was the award's first recipient in 1923–24.

Some NHL trophies are awarded by statistics, like the Art Ross Trophy, which goes to the scoring leader, but most trophy winners are selected by a vote. Members of the Professional Hockey Writers Association vote on many of the trophies, but not all of them. For example, the Vezina Trophy, which goes to the league's best goalie, is selected by the general managers of the 30 NHL teams, and the Jack Adams Award for best coach is selected by members of the NHL Broadcasters' Association.

A Priceless Experience

Kim St-Pierre started playing hockey when she was eight years old. Like many female players, she had to compete against boys. When she was 18 years old, she began playing women's hockey at McGill University in Montreal, and also had a stint on the men's varsity team. She has won three Olympic gold medals and five World Championships, as well as two Clarkson Cups with the Canadian Women's Hockey League's Montreal Stars.

On October 23, 2008, St-Pierre was getting ready for practice with the Stars when she got a call from the Montreal Canadiens. Their goalie Carey Price had the flu, and the Canadiens needed someone to guard one of their nets during practice. St-Pierre became the first woman to stop shots from NHL players since Manon Rheaume played in exhibition games for Tampa Bay in 1992 and 1993.

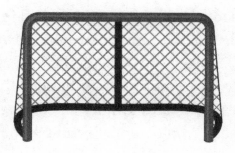

Wayne Gretzky is the only player in NHL history to score more than 200 points in a single season, and he did it four times! Gretzky had 212 points in 1981–82, 205 points in 1983–84, 208 points in 1984–85 and 215 points in 1985–86.

In a Hart Beat

After the 1999–2000 season, Chris Pronger beat Jaromir Jagr for the Hart Trophy by a single point in the voting. At the time, it was the closest vote in the history of the trophy. However, it got even closer: two years later Jose Theodore and Jarome Iginla tied in the voting. Theodore ended up winning the trophy because he had received more first-place votes. Iginla didn't go home from the awards ceremony empty-handed though. He won the Maurice Richard Trophy for scoring 52 goals, and the Art Ross Trophy for collecting 96 points.

Who Was That Lady?

The Lady Byng Trophy is the NHL's second-oldest individual award. It was donated to the league in 1925 and rewards sportsmanship and gentlemanly conduct. Lady Byng's full name and title was Marie Moreton, Viscountess Byng of Vimy. She was married  to Julian Byng, Viscount of Vimy, a British general who commanded the Canadian Army in World War I. Lady Byng donated her trophy to the NHL while her husband was serving as the Governor General of Canada.

The first winner of the Lady Byng Trophy was Ottawa's Frank Nighbor. One year earlier, Nighbor had been the first winner of the Hart Trophy.

Winner-Take-All

In the early days of hockey history, there were no playoffs. Teams that finished in first place in the standings automatically became the champions of their league. A playoff game was only played if one or more teams finished in a tie for first place. Back then, a series for the Stanley Cup wasn't considered to be a playoff the way we think of playoffs today, and it could take place at any time the weather was cold enough for water to freeze into ice: before the season, after the season, or even during the season. Sometimes, teams just played one winner-take-all game for the Stanley Cup. Often, they played a best-of-three series. Other times, teams would play a two-game series. In those cases, the total goals scored in both games were added up to determine who was the overall winner.

Still Growing . . .

In 1948, the Stanley Cup was remodelled into the "barrel shape" we're familiar with today. Since 1958, the barrel of the Stanley Cup has had five large bands for engraving names. Each band can hold 13 years worth of championship team and player names.

Running Out of Room

When the Stanley Cup was remodelled in 1958, the plan was for the space on the five big bands on the base to last through the 1991–92 season — the year that would mark the Stanley Cup's 100th season. Unfortunately, the names of the winners from the Montreal Canadiens in 1964–65 took up too much room. By 1991, the Cup was completely filled. The NHL and the Hockey Hall of Fame gave a lot of thought to what they should do with the Stanley Cup once it was filled. Should they add another band and make it bigger? Or should they start a whole new Stanley Cup?

No one really liked the idea of a new Stanley Cup, but the NHL didn't want to change its shape or make it bigger. The size and shape of the Stanley Cup had become familiar to hockey fans all around the world. The simplest way to keep the Cup the same size was to remove the top band from the barrel (which contained the Cup winners from 1928 to 1940) and retire it to the Hockey Hall of Fame. Then the four remaining bands were moved up the barrel, and a new fifth band was added at the bottom. When this new bottom band was filled after Tampa Bay's victory in 2004, yet another band was removed from the top (1941 to 1953) and another new one was added to the bottom. The newest bottom band will be all filled up in 2017 and the process will have to be repeated again.

Double Size, Triple Loss

The NHL officially added six new teams to the "Original Six" on June 5, 1967. The six new teams were the Philadelphia Flyers, Pittsburgh Penguins, St. Louis Blues, Los Angeles Kings, Minnesota North Stars and Oakland Seals. The NHL now had two divisions. The "Original Six" teams were kept together in the East Division, while the six new teams were in the West Division. To keep things exciting for the fans in new NHL cities, the playoffs were set up so that for the next three years one expansion team and one original team would always meet in the Stanley Cup Finals. In each of those three seasons, the expansion team that reached the Finals was the St. Louis Blues. They didn't do very well once they got there though. The Montreal Canadiens swept St. Louis in four straight games in 1968 and again in 1969. In 1970, St. Louis faced Boston for the Stanley Cup, but the results didn't change. The Bruins also beat the Blues four in a row. In all the years since, the Blues have never made it to the Finals again.

Flying Fast

In 1974, the Philadelphia Flyers were the first of the 1967 expansion teams to win the Stanley Cup. It had only taken them seven seasons to do it, and they followed up that win with another the following year.

Rat Trick

On October 8, 1995, Scott Mellanby of the Florida Panthers used his stick to kill a rat in the dressing room at the Miami Arena. That night, he scored two goals in a 4–3 win over the Calgary Flames. After the game, his teammates kidded him about scoring a "rat trick."

Newspapers reported the joke. After that, every time Mellanby scored a goal, fans threw rubber rats onto the ice. Soon, Florida fans were throwing rats onto the ice whenever anyone on the team scored a goal. It seemed to bring the Panthers good luck. That season, the team went all the way to the Stanley Cup Finals.

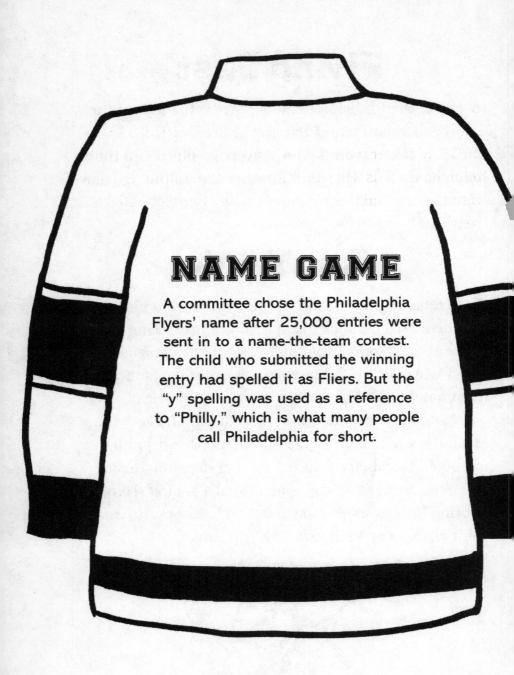

NAME GAME

A committee chose the Philadelphia Flyers' name after 25,000 entries were sent in to a name-the-team contest. The child who submitted the winning entry had spelled it as Fliers. But the "y" spelling was used as a reference to "Philly," which is what many people call Philadelphia for short.

A Real Lady's Man

Frank Boucher was a star player with the New York
Rangers in the 1920s and '30s. Between 1928 and
1935, Boucher won the Lady Byng Trophy seven times
in eight seasons. He won it so many times, the NHL gave
him the original trophy to keep! Lady Byng donated a
new one in 1936.

Masked Marvel

Jacques Plante was one of the best goalies in NHL history. He is also one of the most important. Plante was one of the first goalies to roam outside his crease. He would stop dump-ins behind his net, and he would get loose pucks in front and pass them to his defencemen. Most importantly, Jacques Plante made the goalie mask a standard piece of hockey equipment.

Before Jacques Plante, goalies faced shooters with a bare face. They were often cut and bruised. Some of them lost the sight in an eye after being hit in the face with a puck.

After surgery on his face during the 1957–58 season, Plante began wearing a mask in practice. The management of the Montreal Canadiens didn't want him using his mask in games though. Then, on November 1, 1959, Plante was cut in the face by a shot from Andy Bathgate of the New York Rangers. At this time, NHL teams did not carry more than one goalie, so Plante had to get stitched up and go back into the game. But he refused to unless Canadiens coach Toe Blake let him wear his mask. Plante wore the mask, and the rest is history!

Plante with his mask in a game against Toronto in 1959

About Face

Although Jacques Plante made the goalie mask a standard piece of hockey equipment, he wasn't actually the first goalie to wear a mask in an NHL game. The first was Clint Benedict of the Montreal Maroons. He was hit in the face with shots in back-to-back games on January 4 and January 7, 1930. The second shot resulted in a badly broken nose. Benedict was sidelined for six weeks. When he returned to action on February 20, he wore a mask made of leather. Benedict wore the mask for five games. Unfortunately, on the night of March 4, 1930, an Ottawa player fell on Benedict in a scramble. Benedict's mask pushed down on his face . . . and broke his nose again! Benedict never played another game in the NHL after that night.

But one of the earliest mentions of a goalie wearing

a mask dates back more than 110 years. Eddie Giroux was a goalie with the Toronto Marlboros. During a pre-season practice in Toronto in December 1903, Giroux was hit in the face with a puck. To protect his injury, Giroux began to wear a baseball catcher's mask. Unfortunately, he had trouble following the puck through the bars of the mask. Giroux stopped wearing it before the season started.

The first goalie to wear a mask in an actual game is believed to be Elizabeth Graham. She played with a women's hockey team at Queen's University in Kingston, Ontario. Graham wore her mask in 1927 — three years before Clint Benedict wore his in the NHL. The *Montreal Daily Star* reported that Graham "gave the fans a surprise when she stepped into the net and then donned a fencing mask."

According to stories, Elizabeth Graham's father pressured her into wearing the mask. He'd just paid for her to have expensive dental work.

The Next Six

Six more teams were added to the NHL during the 1970s, bringing the league up to 18 teams. The Buffalo Sabres and Vancouver Canucks joined the league for the 1970–71 season. The Atlanta Flames and New York Islanders came along in 1972–73 and then, in 1974–75, the Washington Capitals and the Colorado Rockies. At first, Buffalo was the best of these new teams. It took the Sabres only five seasons to reach the Stanley Cup Finals, where they lost to Philadelphia in 1975. The New York Islanders started slowly, but they came on fast. They won the Stanley Cup in 1980 after just eight seasons in the league. Not only that, the Islanders went on to win the Cup for four years in a row!

ON THE ROAD WITH STANLEY

In 2014, Alec Martinez scored the Stanley Cup–winning goal in overtime to help the Los Angeles Kings beat the New York Rangers. When he got to spend his day with the Cup that summer, one of the first things he did was fill the bowl with Froot Loops and eat his breakfast.

CUP CHRONICLES

Over the years, many mistakes (and some corrections) have been made in the names engraved on the Stanley Cup. Here's a look at some of the strangest:

1937–38: Chicago Black Hawks

Pete Palangio had his name engraved twice. One time, it's spelled correctly. The other time it's spelled P-A-L-A-G-I-O.

1941–42: Toronto Maple Leafs

Maple Leafs goalie Turk Broda is listed twice. One time, he's engraved as TURK BRODA. The other time, his real name of WALTER BRODA appears on the Cup.

1951–52: Detroit Red Wings

Two mistakes were made this year. Coach Tommy Ivan is engraved as TOMMY NIVAN. Alex Delvecchio's last name is misspelled as BELVECCHIO.

1953, 1956–60: Montreal Canadiens

Dickie Moore won the Stanley Cup six times and his named is spelled five different ways: DICKIE MOORE, D MOORE, RICH MOORE, RICHARD MOORE (his real first name) and R MOORE.

1956–60: Montreal Canadiens
Montreal won the Stanley Cup five years in a row, and Jacques Plante's name is spelled four different ways: J PLANTE, JACQUES PLANTE, JAC PLANTE, and JACQ PLANTE.

1962–63: Toronto Maple Leafs
The team name is misspelled as TORONTO MAPLE LEAES.

1971–72: Boston Bruins
Misspelled as BQSTQN BRUINS.

1976–77: Montreal Canadiens
Bob Gainey's first name is listed as ROBERT (his real name) and his last name as GAINY.

1980–81: New York Islanders
Misspelled as NEW YORK ILANDERS.

1983–84: Edmonton Oilers
Oilers owner Peter Pocklington thought it would be a nice touch to have his father's name engraved on the Stanley Cup next to his . . . even though his father had nothing to do with the team. The NHL disagreed. So where the name BASIL POCKLINGTON briefly appeared, there is now XXXXX XXXXXXXXXXX.

1995–96: *Colorado Avalanche*

Adam Deadmarsh was misspelled as ADAM DEADMARCH. Later, this mistake was corrected. It was the first time a correction was made to a misspelled name on the Stanley Cup. But not the last!

2001–02: *Detroit Red Wings*

MANNY LAGACE was corrected to MANNY LEGACE.

2005–06: *Carolina Hurricanes*

ERIC STAAAL was corrected to ERIC STAAL.

2009–10: *Chicago Blackhawks*

KRIS VERTSEEG was corrected to KRIS VERSTEEG.

DID YOU KNOW?

On January 7, 1981, Marcel Dionne of the Los Angeles Kings scored the fastest 1,000 points in NHL history, doing it in 740 games. Wayne Gretzky later crushed the record, reaching 1,000 points in just 424 games on December 19, 1984.

Stanley's Cups

Over the years, almost all of the pieces of the Stanley Cup have had to be replaced. The original bowl had become very fragile by 1968, so a new bowl, designed to look exactly like the original, was made. It has been sitting atop the trophy since 1970. Other pieces have had to be replaced too.

Though it no longer has all its original parts, it is still the "real" Stanley Cup that is presented to teams on the ice and that travels with players after they win it. This "Presentation Cup" travels for more than 300 days a year to be displayed at hospitals, charity fundraisers, NHL arenas, hockey rinks, players' hometowns and other venues.

Before the Hockey Hall of Fame moved to its present location in 1993, the Hall had nothing to display when the Stanley Cup was on the road. When the Hall of Fame moved, it had a new version of the Stanley Cup built. This replica of the Cup goes on display at the Hall whenever the real Cup has to be somewhere else. So nowadays, there are actually three Stanley Cups in existence: the original bowl, the Presentation Cup and the replica Cup.

East Is East, and West Is . . . East?

Everyone knows that Vancouver is on Canada's west coast. Still, when the Canucks joined the NHL in 1970, they were put in the East Division and played there for four years. It seems strange, but the NHL thought having Vancouver in the East gave the divisions a better balance of old teams and expansion teams.

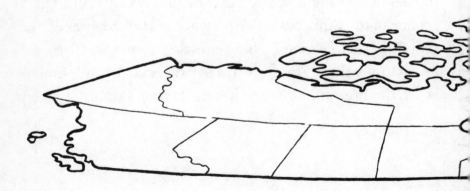

Supporting the Troops

Hockey has always meant a lot to Canadians and the men and women serving in the military abroad. In both World War I and World War II, many Canadian hockey players left their teams to serve. Some players were even killed in battle, like Ottawa star Frank McGee and Scotty Davidson, who won the Stanley Cup with the Toronto Blueshirts in 1914.

By the start of the 1942–43 season, so many hockey players had joined the Armed Forces to serve in World War II that the NHL considered suspending play. However, the government asked the NHL to keep hockey going. It was thought that game would be good for the morale of the soldiers, as well as the people on the home front.

Hockey is still very important to Canadian soldiers serving overseas. On May 2, 2007, the Stanley Cup arrived in Kandahar, Afghanistan, on a Canadian Forces C–130 Hercules transport plane. The next day, 17 former NHL players played a ball hockey game against Canadian soldiers on a concrete rink in the Afghan desert.

More than just Canadian soldiers were pleased with the Stanley Cup's visit to Afghanistan. A stop was also made at a nearby American army base, and troops from Sweden, the United Kingdom, Slovakia, the Czech Republic and elsewhere were all excited to see the historic trophy on display. The Stanley Cup made a second trip to Afghanistan for a four-day visit in March of 2008 and returned once again in 2010.

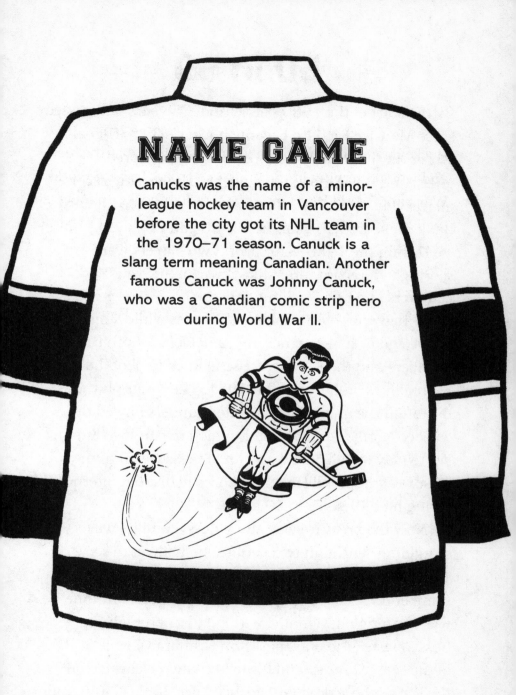

NAME GAME

Canucks was the name of a minor-league hockey team in Vancouver before the city got its NHL team in the 1970–71 season. Canuck is a slang term meaning Canadian. Another famous Canuck was Johnny Canuck, who was a Canadian comic strip hero during World War II.

50 in 50

By the start of the 1980–81 season, 35 years had passed since Maurice Richard became hockey's first 50-goal-scorer. In that time, 23 more players had scored 50 goals, and Phil Esposito had pushed the scoring record all the way up to 76. Still, no one but Maurice Richard had ever scored 50 goals in just 50 games played.

During the 1980–81 season, two players were scoring at a record rate: Mike Bossy of the New York Islanders and Charlie Simmer of the Los Angeles Kings. Bossy had scored 48 goals in 49 games while Simmer had 46 goals in 49 games. By coincidence, both the Islanders and the Kings were scheduled to play their 50th games on January 24, 1981. The Kings played Boston in the afternoon, and the Islanders played the Quebec Nordiques that night, which meant that Simmer got to play first. There was a lot of pressure on him, and he sure came close! He scored three goals that afternoon, giving him 49 goals in 50 games.

Now the pressure was all on Bossy, and he was struggling. Through two periods, he had yet to score. Then, with only 4:10 to go in the game, he scored number 49. Bossy continued to get chances, but time was running out. Finally, with just 1:29 remaining, Bossy blasted the puck past Ron Grahame for his 50th of the season. Bossy and his teammates celebrated on the ice, as the scoreboard flashed "50! 50! 50! 50!" And Simmer? He scored his 50th two days later, in game number 51.

Bossy celebrates his 50th goal in 1981.

Mike Bossy was the first player in NHL history to score 50 goals in his rookie season. He did it with 53 goals for the Islanders in 1977–78.

Junior Achievement

Though it's officially known as the World Under-20 Championship, most Canadians know this tournament as the World Junior Championship. Today, it's a holiday tradition for many Canadian hockey fans over the Christmas season. Every year millions tune in to watch the tournament on TV.

The plan to create a World Junior Championship began in 1973. Three unofficial tournaments were held before the event truly got under way in the winter of 1976–77.

Finally, in 1981–82, the idea of a national junior team was born. There were no playoffs at the tournament back then. Eight teams took part, and each one played each of the other seven teams once. The medals were determined by the standings. That first year Canada won six of its seven games, and tied one. The team's biggest win was a 7–0 victory over the Soviet Union. Including the unofficial events, the Soviets had won the Junior title seven times in a row from 1974 to 1980. Since winning the event for the first time in 1982, Canada has won more gold medals at the World Junior Championship than any other country.

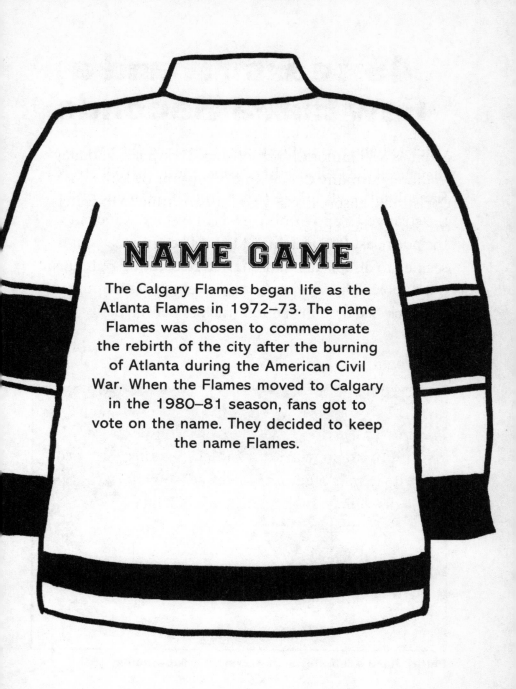

NAME GAME

The Calgary Flames began life as the Atlanta Flames in 1972–73. The name Flames was chosen to commemorate the rebirth of the city after the burning of Atlanta during the American Civil War. When the Flames moved to Calgary in the 1980–81 season, fans got to vote on the name. They decided to keep the name Flames.

49 Years . . . and a Few Extra Seconds

Chicago hadn't won the Stanley Cup since 1961 when they faced the Philadelphia Flyers in June 2010. Patrick Kane finally ended the 49-year drought with one of the strangest Cup-winning goals in history. Kane put the puck past Philadelphia's Michael Leighton . . . but it seemed to disappear! Kane started celebrating right away, but it took a bit longer for everyone else to figure out that the puck had actually gotten stuck under the net.

Patrick Kane celebrates after scoring his Cup-winning goal.

BY THE NUMBERS

NHL teams with the longest current Stanley Cup winless streaks:

Team	Last Win
Toronto Maple Leafs	1967
Philadelphia Flyers	1975
New York Islanders	1982
Calgary Flames	1989
Edmonton Oilers	1990

The Great One

Wayne Gretzky was born to be a hockey star. He learned to skate when he was two years old, and practised on a rink in his backyard. By the time he was six years old, he was playing on a hockey team with boys who were 10. When he was 10, Gretzky scored 378 goals in a single season.

Gretzky signed his first professional hockey contract when he was just 17 years old. Players that young are not allowed to play in the NHL. Instead, he signed with a new rival league called the World Hockey Association. Although he played with men much older than he was, Gretzky was one of the WHA's top scorers.

The next year, in 1979–80, four WHA teams joined the NHL. Gretzky's Edmonton Oilers were one of those four teams. People believed that Gretzky wouldn't do as well in the NHL as he had in the WHA. They thought he was too young and too small to succeed. Were they ever wrong! In his first season, Gretzky scored 51 goals. He also had 86 assists for a total of 137 points.

In his second NHL season, Gretzky got 109 assists, breaking Bobby Orr's record of 102 in a single year. Combined with his 55 goals, that gave him 164 points to break Phil Esposito's record of 152. Over the years, Gretzky would continue to break records. He pushed the assist mark from 109 to 120 to 125 to 135, then finally to 163. No one has ever broken that record. Gretzky also pushed the points record from 164 all the way to 215, a record that still stands to this day. Not bad for someone who was too young and too small.

Team captains have been part of hockey since the game's earliest days. In 1946, the NHL enacted Rule 14a, which required the captain to wear a "C" on the front of his uniform. Alternate captains are required to wear an "A." The captain or alternate captains are the only players on the ice who are allowed to talk to the referee.

Swimming Lessons?

After the Pittsburgh Penguins won the Stanley Cup for the first time in 1991, captain Mario Lemieux invited all the players over to his house for a party. Everyone was having a lot of fun and fooling around, and at one point the Stanley Cup got thrown into Lemieux's pool. It quickly sank to the bottom. The same thing happened in 1993 when Patrick Roy held a party for his Montreal Canadiens teammates. The strange thing is, when Mario Lemieux (now the team's owner) hosted a party for the Penguins in 2009, the Stanley Cup wound up in his pool once again . . . but this time, it seemed to float. Maybe it was all those swimming lessons!

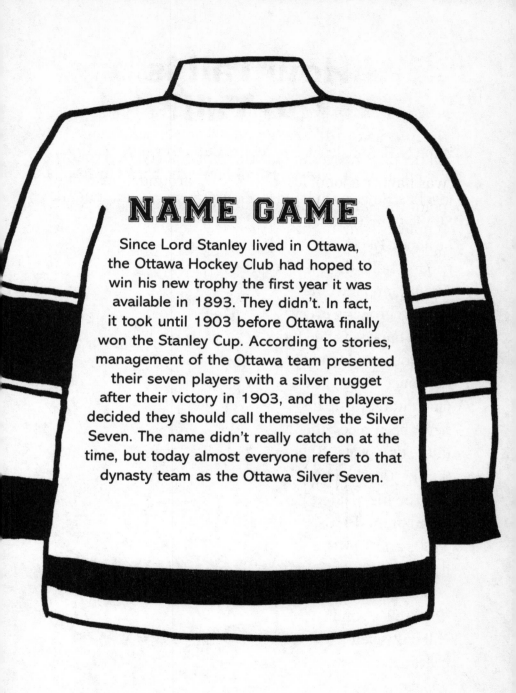

NAME GAME

Since Lord Stanley lived in Ottawa, the Ottawa Hockey Club had hoped to win his new trophy the first year it was available in 1893. They didn't. In fact, it took until 1903 before Ottawa finally won the Stanley Cup. According to stories, management of the Ottawa team presented their seven players with a silver nugget after their victory in 1903, and the players decided they should call themselves the Silver Seven. The name didn't really catch on at the time, but today almost everyone refers to that dynasty team as the Ottawa Silver Seven.

How Tall Is Too Tall?

If the NHL had decided to let the Cup grow back in 1992, it would now have seven bands down the barrel instead of just five. Since each band is about 9.5 cm (3.7 in.) tall, the Stanley Cup would be about 19 cm (7.5 in.) taller than it is today, and it would keep on growing every time a band gets filled. But what would have happened if the "stove pipe" Stanley Cup had never been redesigned in the first place? If the Stanley Cup had kept on growing just like it had in the 1920s, 1930s and 1940s, it would now be about 2.7 metres (9 ft.) tall . . . and still only a few centimetres wide!

Inside and Out

According to most sources, Phil Bourque was the one who threw the Stanley Cup into Mario Lemieux's swimming pool back in 1991. But Bourque has another claim to fame. He is the only player who has his name engraved on the outside of the Stanley Cup and on the inside. Apparently, Bourque heard a rattling noise coming from inside the Cup and tried to fix it himself. He pried off the bottom of the Cup with a screwdriver and noticed there were a few names on the inside. So Bourque decided to scratch his own message there: "Enjoy it, Phil Bubba Bourque, '91 Penguins."

March a Hero in April

Patrick Kane is not the only Chicago player to win the Stanley Cup in overtime. On April 10, 1934, the Black Hawks won their very first Stanley Cup with a goal in sudden death. Harold "Mush" March scored at 10:05 of the second overtime period to give Chicago a 1–0 Stanley Cup victory over Detroit.

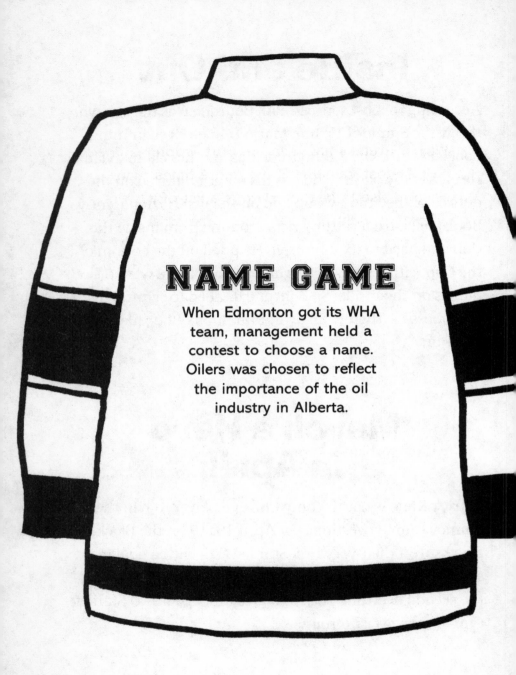

NAME GAME

When Edmonton got its WHA team, management held a contest to choose a name. Oilers was chosen to reflect the importance of the oil industry in Alberta.

BY THE NUMBERS

Wayne Gretzky has won the Hart Trophy as the NHL's Most Valuable Player more times than anyone else in history. Here is a list of players who have won the Hart Trophy the most times:

Player	Wins
Wayne Gretzky	9
Gordie Howe	6
Eddie Shore	4
Mario Lemieux	3
Bobby Clarke	3
Bobby Orr	3
Howie Morenz	3
Alex Ovechkin	3

Not just anyone can be a team captain. Few NHL teams have ever had a playing coach, but if they did, that player couldn't be captain. Goalies aren't supposed to be captains either. The rule (Rule 6.1) against goalies being captains was passed in 1948 because people thought it would take too much time for a goalie to leave his crease to discuss things with the referee. However, the Vancouver Canucks made Roberto Luongo their captain in 2008–09. He was the first goalie to be a captain since Bill Durnan of the Montreal Canadiens in 1947–48. Still, Luongo was not allowed to wear the "C" on his sweater.

BY THE NUMBERS

Here's a look at some of the top single-season goal scorers in NHL history:

Goals	Player	Team	Season
92	Wayne Gretzky	Edmonton	1981–82
87	Wayne Gretzky	Edmonton	1983–84
86	Brett Hull	St. Louis	1990–91
85	Mario Lemieux	Pittsburgh	1988–89
76	Phil Esposito	Boston	1970–71
76	Alexander Mogilny	Buffalo	1992–93
76	Teemu Selanne	Winnipeg	1992–93
73	Wayne Gretzky	Edmonton	1984–85

Making Their Marks

The names Phil Bourque saw inside the Stanley Cup
back in 1991 were probably the names of the people
who have engraved the trophy over the years. Since the
1940s, only four different people have officially had the
job of engraving names on the Stanley Cup.

The first was a silversmith named Carl Petersen,
who came to Montreal from Denmark in 1929. He
engraved the names on the Cup from the 1940s until
his death in 1977. After that, his son Arno engraved
the Cup for a couple of years until he decided to close
his father's business. (Over the years, two men named
Ernie Phillips and Fred Light used to help the Petersens
with the engraving.) In 1979, Doug Boffey took over the
engraving job. Since 1989, Louise St. Jacques of Boffey
Promotions Ltd. has been the only one engraving names
onto the Stanley Cup.

Although the word "engraved" is always used to
describe how the names get put on the Stanley Cup,
the truth is that they're actually stamped on. Special
hammers of different weights are used to strike against
a letter-punch to sink each letter (they're all capitals)
into the silver. An extra piece of metal temporarily holds
a line in place to make sure the names go on as straight
and level as possible. Each name takes about half an
hour to complete.

ON THE ROAD WITH STANLEY

The Stanley Cup added a new country to its travel itinerary when Anze Kopitar of the Los Angeles Kings brought the trophy to his native Slovenia in 2012. This was the 24th different country the Cup had visited. It returned to Slovenia in 2014 when Kopitar and the Kings won the Stanley Cup for the second time.

On March 21, 1998, South Korea defeated Thailand 92–0 on the last day of the Asia-Oceania Under-18 Championships in Harbin, China. This is the highest-scoring game in any tournament ever organized by the International Ice Hockey Federation.

D'oh!

Wayne Gretzky played in 49 different arenas during his NHL career. He had at least one point in 48 of them. Which arena saw Gretzky go pointless? The Springfield Civic Center. The Civic Center in Springfield, Massachusetts, was the home of the Hartford Whalers for the first four months of the 1979–80 season. After that, the Whalers moved back to the Civic Center in Hartford, Connecticut.

Gretzky's 50

In 1981–82, Wayne Gretzky smashed the marks of Maurice Richard and Mike Bossy for 50 goals in 50 games. On December 30, 1981, in just his 39th game, Gretzky scored his 50th goal of the season: he'd scored five goals that night to break the record. But Gretzky didn't stop there. He went on to break Phil Esposito's single-season record of 76 goals. He did that in his 64th game on February 24, 1982, when he scored three goals. Gretzky continued to push the record all the way up to 92 goals. Like his records for points and assists, no one has broken Gretzky's goal-scoring record either.

DID YOU KNOW?

*The longest winning streak and the
longest losing streak in NHL history
both lasted 17 games. Two different
teams have had losing streaks of 17
in a row. The first was the Washington
Capitals, who lost 17 straight from
February 18 to March 26, 1975.
Then, in 1993, the San Jose Sharks
lost 17 in a row from January 4
to February 12. As for the longest
winning streak? That belongs to the
Pittsburgh Penguins, who won 17
straight games from March 9 to
April 10, 1993.*

Knight Shines in Anaheim

On October 3, 2014, the Anaheim Ducks invited two-time Olympic silver medalist Hilary Knight to practise with them. The 25-year-old female phenom got on the ice with the Ducks to help promote World Girls' Ice Hockey Weekend. It's believed to be the first time a woman other than a goalie has ever practised with an NHL team. Knight is a member of the United States Women's National Team and also skates for the Boston Blades, who play in the Canadian Women's Hockey League. Standing 1.80 m (5 ft., 11 in.) tall, she's one of the biggest players in women's hockey. Her size and speed fit in nicely at the Ducks practice.

"Once she got over the jitters, I think she was really good," said Ducks coach Bruce Boudreau. "I'd be pretty nervous if I walked into an NHL room and had to practise with them, and I thought she handled it really well."

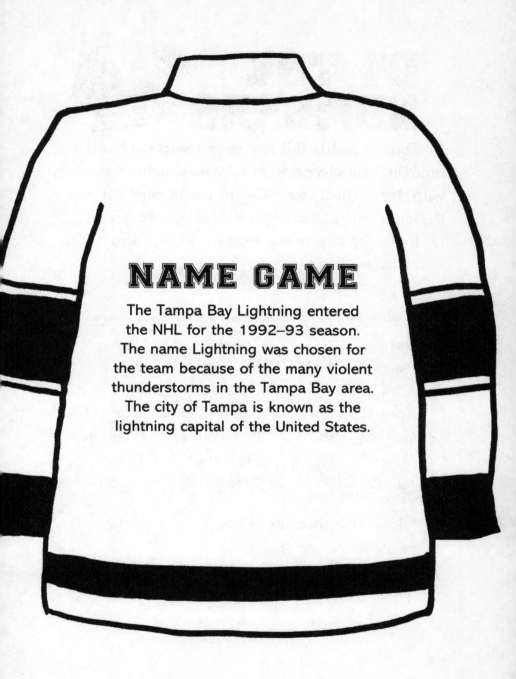

NAME GAME

The Tampa Bay Lightning entered
the NHL for the 1992–93 season.
The name Lightning was chosen for
the team because of the many violent
thunderstorms in the Tampa Bay area.
The city of Tampa is known as the
lightning capital of the United States.

BY THE NUMBERS

The biggest deficit any team has come back from to win a game in a Stanley Cup series is three goals. Six different teams have come back from either down 3–0 or 4–1 to win a Stanley Cup game. Here's a look at the complete list:

Date	Teams
March 29, 1919	Montreal 4, Seattle 3
April 9, 1936	Toronto 4, Detroit 3
April 13, 1944	Montreal 5, Chicago 4 (OT)*
May 22, 1987	Philadelphia 5, Edmonton 3
May 26, 1992	Pittsburgh 5, Chicago 4†
June 5, 2006	Carolina 5, Edmonton 4†

*victory clinched the series
†went on to win the series

Just Two, Not Three

In the early days of hockey, games had two 30-minute halves instead of three periods. The switch to three 20-minute periods was made before the 1910–11 season. The first Stanley Cup game with three periods instead of two halves was played on March 13, 1911, between the Ottawa Senators and the Galt Professionals.

Game

Game 5

Game 3

Game 4

Game 3

Game 1

Game 1

Captain Kid: Part I

Vincent Lecavalier was named captain of the Tampa Bay Lightning on March 3, 2000, when he was just 19 years and 11 months old. At the time, that made Lecavalier the youngest captain in NHL history. However, after the 2000–01 season, the Lightning took the "C" away. They decided that being such a young captain put too much pressure on Lecavalier. Maybe they were right, as Lecavalier went on to become a big star in the NHL.

Rookie Rewards

The NHL has been rewarding its Rookie of the Year since 1933. From 1937 until his death in 1943, NHL president Frank Calder would buy a new trophy every year. After his death, the NHL presented a permanent trophy, which they named the Calder Memorial Trophy.

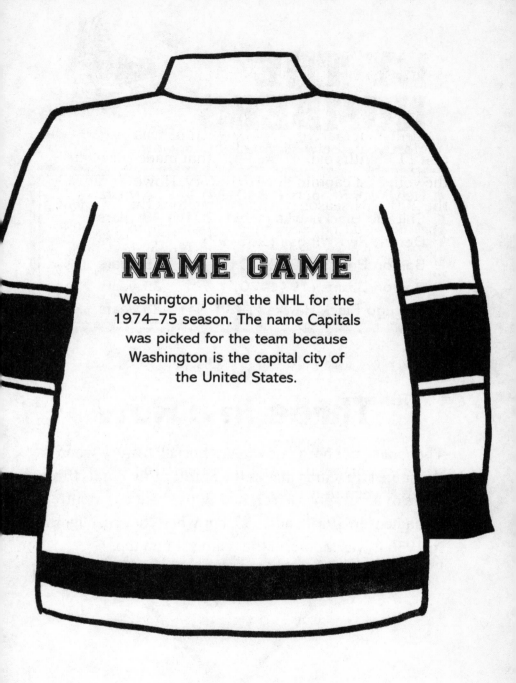

NAME GAME

Washington joined the NHL for the 1974–75 season. The name Capitals was picked for the team because Washington is the capital city of the United States.

BY THE NUMBERS

Most years between Stanley Cup wins:

New York Rangers (1940–94)	54 years
Chicago Blackhawks (1961–2010)	49 years
Detroit Red Wings (1955–97)	42 years
Boston Bruins (1972–2011)	39 years
Boston Bruins (1941–70)	29 years
Chicago Black Hawks (1938–61)	23 years

Three in a Row

There has only been one time in hockey history when the same two teams met in the Stanley Cup Finals three years in a row. The Detroit Red Wings beat the Montreal Canadiens in 1954 and 1955, but when they met again in 1956 it was Montreal that came out on top.

Dan the Man

On January 31, 1901, Dan Bain, one of Canada's finest athletes, became the first player in hockey history to score the Stanley Cup–winning goal in overtime. Bain scored four minutes into the sudden death period to give the Winnipeg Victorias a 2–1 victory over the Montreal Shamrocks.

Two of a Kind

Only twice in history has the seventh game of the Stanley Cup Finals been decided in overtime. The winner in both cases was the Detroit Red Wings. In 1950, Pete Babando scored at 8:31 of double overtime to give Detroit a 4–3 win over the New York Rangers. Four years later, in 1954, Tony Leswick's long shot bounced off Montreal defenceman Doug Harvey and past goalie Gerry McNeil. The fluky goal gave the Red Wings a 2–1 win over the Canadiens at 4:20 of overtime.

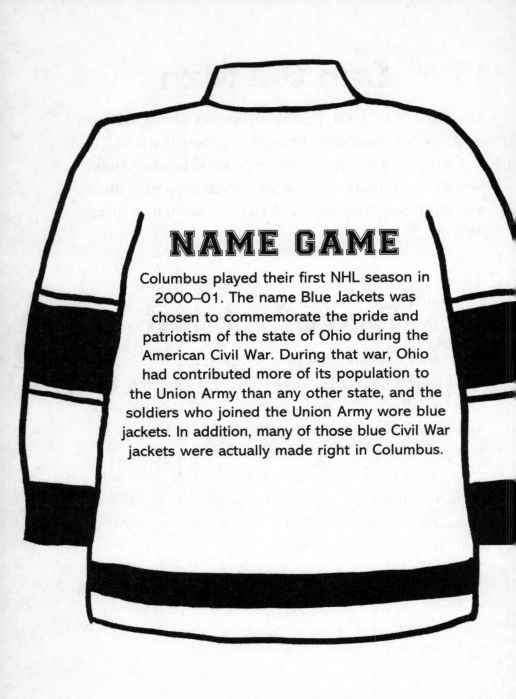

NAME GAME

Columbus played their first NHL season in 2000–01. The name Blue Jackets was chosen to commemorate the pride and patriotism of the state of Ohio during the American Civil War. During that war, Ohio had contributed more of its population to the Union Army than any other state, and the soldiers who joined the Union Army wore blue jackets. In addition, many of those blue Civil War jackets were actually made right in Columbus.

Mario the Magnificent

Mario Lemieux was a star player. He was chosen first overall by the Pittsburgh Penguins in the 1984 draft. In just his second season, he finished second behind Wayne Gretzky in the league scoring race. Even after suffering a serious back injury in the 1989–90 season, he led the Penguins to their first Stanley Cup Championship. But then on January 12, 1993, the Penguins announced that Mario had Hodgkin's Disease, a form of cancer. He had to leave the team to get therapy.

Lemieux's cancer treatments — which are very tiring — lasted from February 1 to March 2. But on the very day he finished his treatment, Lemieux returned to action with the Penguins.

Before getting sick, Lemieux had collected 104 points in just 40 games. He was 20 points in front in the NHL scoring race. However, he'd missed 20 games while he was sick. By March 7, Pat LaFontaine, Adam Oates and Steve Yzerman had all passed him in the scoring race. LaFontaine was the leader now, and he was 16 points ahead of Lemieux.

Sick as he'd been, no one expected that Lemieux could possibly catch up. But he did. He scored 30 goals and got 26 assists in the last 20 games of the season. He finished the year with just 60 games played, but had 69 goals and 91 assists for 160 points. LaFontaine, Oates and Yzerman had each played 24 more games than Lemieux, but he had passed them all. Lemieux won the race for the Art Ross Trophy by 12 points. And once again, he won the Hart Trophy.

Gone Fishin'

When Bryan Bickell won the Stanley Cup with the
Blackhawks in 2010, he came up with a brand new idea
for celebrating with it. Bickell was an avid fisherman and
he wanted to be the first person to put a fish in the Stanley
Cup. Bickell put a life jacket on the Stanley Cup, loaded it
onto his boat, and went fishing. He didn't catch anything,
but his girlfriend did, and her small silver-scaled bass fit
very nicely into the silver Stanley Cup bowl.

BY THE NUMBERS

NHL teams that have never won the Stanley Cup:

Team	First NHL Season
St. Louis Blues	1967–1968
Buffalo Sabres	1970–1971
Vancouver Canucks	1970–1971
Washington Capitals	1974–1975
Arizona Coyotes	
(formerly Winnipeg Jets)	1979–1980
San Jose Sharks	1991–1992
Ottawa Senators*	1992–1993
Florida Panthers	1993–1994
Nashville Predators	1998–1999
Winnipeg Jets	
(formerly Atlanta Thrashers)	1999–2000
Columbus Blue Jackets	2000–2001
Minnesota Wild	2000–2001

*The Original Ottawa Senators played in the NHL from 1917–1918 to 1933–1934 and won the Stanley Cup in 1920, 1921, 1923 and 1927.

Toronto's Ace

Irvine "Ace" Bailey joined Toronto's hockey team in 1926–27 and quickly became one of the team's top stars. He led the NHL in both goals and points in 1928–29, and in 1932 helped the Leafs win their first Stanley Cup.

On December 12, 1933, Toronto played in Boston. During the second period, Boston's Eddie Shore hit Bailey from behind. At the time, players didn't wear helmets, and Bailey hit his head on the ice, suffering a fractured skull. Two operations saved his life, but he would never play hockey again.

On February 14, 1934, the NHL held a special game to raise money for Bailey. The Maple Leafs played against a team of NHL All-Stars that featured Eddie Shore. Bailey didn't hold him responsible for his accident, and when he shook Shore's hand before the game, Maple Leaf Gardens erupted in cheers. Then it was announced that the Leafs were going to retire Bailey's number 6. He was the first player in NHL history to be given this honour. No Leaf was ever supposed to wear his number again, but before the 1968–69 season, Bailey asked that his number 6 be given to Ron Ellis.

NAME GAME

In the 1912–13 season, two Toronto teams joined the National Hockey Association: the Toronto Tecumsehs and the Toronto Blueshirts. The Blueshirts were often just called the Torontos. When the NHL was formed, control of the Toronto team was given to the Toronto Arena Company. So Toronto's first NHL team was known as the Toronto Arenas. In 1920, the team became known as the Toronto St. Patricks. In February 1927, Conn Smythe bought the team. Smythe changed the team's name to the Toronto Maple Leafs for a couple of reasons. One was that the 1924 Canadian Olympic hockey team had worn a maple leaf on their sweaters. The other was that Canadian soldiers fighting in World War I had worn maple leaf insignias on their uniforms.

BY THE NUMBERS

Here's a look at all 17 players in NHL history who have scored the Stanley Cup–winning goal in overtime:

Year	Player	Team
2014	Alec Martinez	Los Angeles Kings
2010	Patrick Kane	Chicago Blackhawks
2000	Jason Arnott	New Jersey Devils
1999	Brett Hull	Dallas Stars
1996	Uwe Krupp	Colorado Avalanche
1980	Bob Nystrom	NY Islanders
1977	Jacques Lemaire	Montreal Canadiens
1970	Bobby Orr	Boston Bruins
1966	Henri Richard	Montreal Canadiens
1954	Tony Leswick	Detroit Red Wings
1953	Elmer Lach	Montreal Canadiens
1951	Bill Barilko	Toronto Maple Leafs
1950	Pete Babando	Detroit Red Wings
1944	Toe Blake	Montreal Canadiens
1940	Bryan Hextall	NY Rangers
1934	Harold March	Chicago Black Hawks
1933	Bill Cook	NY Rangers

Time	Period	Score	Series
14:43	2OT	3–2	4–1
4:06	OT	4–3	4–2
8:20	2OT	2–1	4–2
14:51	3OT	3–2	4–2
4:31	3OT	1–0	4–0
7:11	OT	5–4	4–2
4:32	OT	2–1	4–0
0:40	OT	4–3	4–0
2:20	OT	3–2	4–2
4:20	OT	2–1	4–3
1:22	OT	1–0	4–1
2:53	OT	3–2	4–1
8:31	2OT	4–3	4–3
9:12	OT	5–4	4–0
2:07	OT	3–2	4–2
10:05	2OT	1–0	3–1
7:34	OT	1–0	3–1

The Penguins Win the Lottery

The order of selection at the NHL Entry Draft is based on the NHL standings. To make sure that nobody tries to finish last just to get the first draft pick, a lottery is used. Still, the worse that a team does, the more chances it has of picking first.

But what happens if there aren't any NHL standings? That happened in 2005. The 2004–05 season had been cancelled by a lockout. Some believed the NHL should just use the same order from the 2004 Draft. Others thought there should be a new lottery based on the standings from the 2003–04 season. But that would mean only five teams had a chance to get the top pick . . . and everyone knew that the top pick in 2005 was going to be Sidney Crosby. Every team wanted a chance to draft him.

So the NHL came up with a lottery system that was fair to everyone. The Penguins — which had been one of the league's worst teams — won and picked Crosby.

Saturday Night Is Hockey Night

Hockey Night in Canada is the longest-running show on Canadian television. The Canadian Broadcasting Corporation (CBC) first showed a hockey game on TV on Saturday, October 11, 1952, between the Detroit Red Wings and the Montreal Canadiens.

The Toronto Maple Leafs made their first appearance on *Hockey Night in Canada* three weeks later, on November 1, 1952.

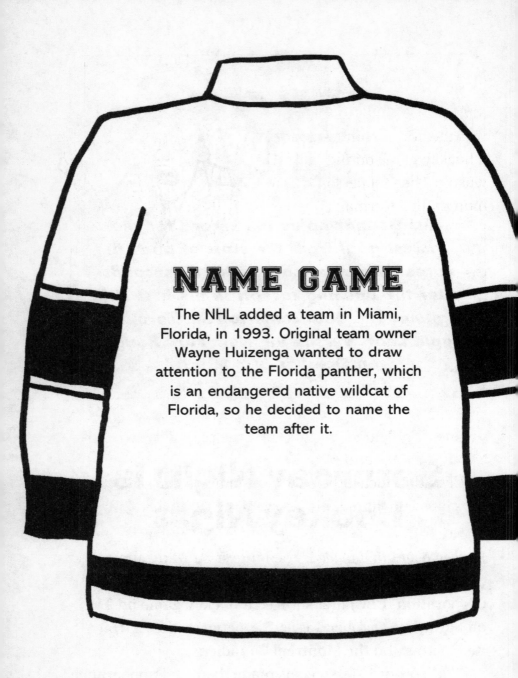

NAME GAME

The NHL added a team in Miami, Florida, in 1993. Original team owner Wayne Huizenga wanted to draw attention to the Florida panther, which is an endangered native wildcat of Florida, so he decided to name the team after it.

On the Air

Most people think that Foster Hewitt was the first person to broadcast a hockey game on the radio. He wasn't. The first person was a man named Norman Albert.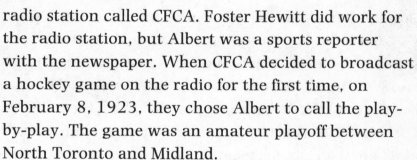

Both Albert and Hewitt worked for the *Toronto Star*. During the 1920s and '30s, the *Star* owned a Toronto radio station called CFCA. Foster Hewitt did work for the radio station, but Albert was a sports reporter with the newspaper. When CFCA decided to broadcast a hockey game on the radio for the first time, on February 8, 1923, they chose Albert to call the play-by-play. The game was an amateur playoff between North Toronto and Midland.

CFCA broadcast the first NHL game on the radio six days later. It was a game between the Ottawa Senators and Toronto St. Patricks. Though it's not known for sure, Albert was probably the broadcaster that night too.

Foster's First

When Foster Hewitt talked about his first radio broadcast, he always said that it was on March 22, 1923. He usually said that it was a semifinal playoff game between the Kitchener Greenshirts and the Parkdale Canoe Club of Toronto. The winner would face the Toronto Granites in the Eastern Canada final.

But there are two problems with Foster Hewitt's story. First, Kitchener and Parkdale never played a game that night. Second, by March 22, 1923, the Toronto Granites had already won the amateur championship.

Later in his life, Foster Hewitt admitted that his memory of the two teams might have been wrong. "I know Kitchener played," he said. "But it may well have been against the Toronto Argonauts." (Back then, the Toronto Argonauts had an amateur hockey team as well as a Canadian football team.)

It turns out that the Toronto Argonauts played a hockey game against the Kitchener Greenshirts on February 16, 1923. This is the game where Foster Hewitt made his first broadcast. His call of the play-by-play was so popular that he soon became a full-time radio sports announcer.

Foster Hewitt lived from 1902 to 1985, but he is probably still the most famous sports broadcaster in Canadian history.

Radio Days

CFCA broadcasts in 1923 only covered the third period and any overtime periods. The first radio station to carry a complete hockey broadcast was CJCG in Winnipeg. That station aired all 60 minutes of an amateur playoff game between the Winnipeg Falcons and the Port Arthur Bearcats on February 22, 1923.

CKCK in Regina was the first radio station to broadcast a full professional hockey game, on March 14, 1923. The game was the first of a Western Canada Hockey League playoff series between the Regina Capitals and the Edmonton Eskimos.

Huselius Hat Trick

Though he's now retired from the NHL, Kristian Huselius began his career with the Florida Panthers with his own unique version of a hat trick. In the first game of the 2001–02 season, Huselius scored the first goal of his career on his very first shot in the NHL. A year later, he did it again: he scored a goal on his very first shot in the very first game of the 2002–03 season. He made it three in a row in 2003–04 when he once again scored a goal on his first shot of the season! That was the end of his first-game scoring streak though. However, in his first game for the Calgary Flames in 2005–06, Huselius did pick up three assists.

Third Time's the Charm

Marian Hossa broke into the NHL with the Ottawa Senators in 1997–98. It took him 10 years to reach the Stanley Cup Finals, but he finally made it with the Pittsburgh Penguins in 2008. Unfortunately for Hossa, the Penguins lost the Stanley Cup to Detroit that year. After the season, Hossa became a free agent and signed a contract with the Red Wings. Detroit made it back to the Finals in 2009 but lost the Stanley Cup . . . to Hossa's old teammates from Pittsburgh. The next year, Hossa was a member of the Chicago Blackhawks. When Chicago reached the Stanley Cup Finals in 2010, Hossa became the first player in NHL history to make it to the Finals with three different teams in three straight years. This time, he finally won it!

On February 16, 2001, Mathieu Schneider became the first defenceman to score a goal against all 30 teams in the NHL after he scored to help Los Angeles beat Minnesota 4–0.

Overtime After Time

The 1951 Stanley Cup Finals between the Toronto Maple Leafs and Montreal Canadiens marks the only playoff series in NHL history where every game went into overtime. Toronto took the series in five games.

Jack Marshall is the only player in hockey history to win the Stanley Cup with four different teams. Marshall played his entire career before the NHL was formed in 1917 and won championships with the 1901 Winnipeg Victorias, the 1902 and 1903 Montreal AAA, the 1907 and 1910 Montreal Wanderers and the 1914 Toronto Blueshirts.

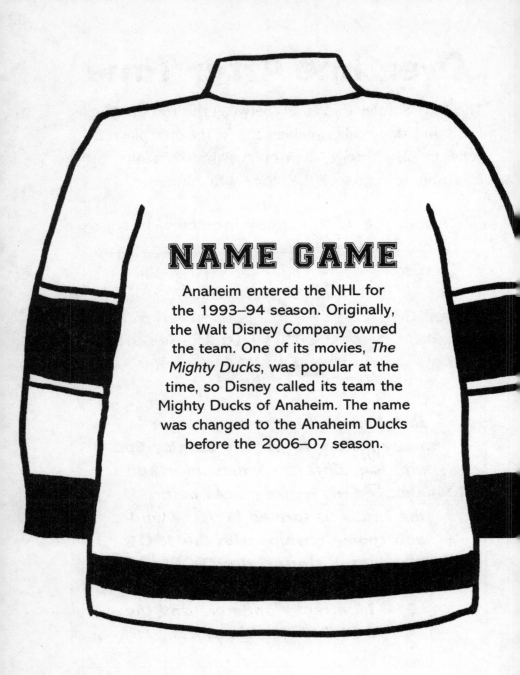

NAME GAME

Anaheim entered the NHL for the 1993–94 season. Originally, the Walt Disney Company owned the team. One of its movies, *The Mighty Ducks*, was popular at the time, so Disney called its team the Mighty Ducks of Anaheim. The name was changed to the Anaheim Ducks before the 2006–07 season.

DID YOU KNOW?

During the 1990s, many northern-based teams moved south. Teams in Minnesota, Quebec, Winnipeg and Hartford moved to Dallas, Colorado, Arizona and Carolina. When the NHL had 21 teams, seven were in Canada and 14 were in the United States. Now that the NHL has 30 teams, there are still only seven in Canada.

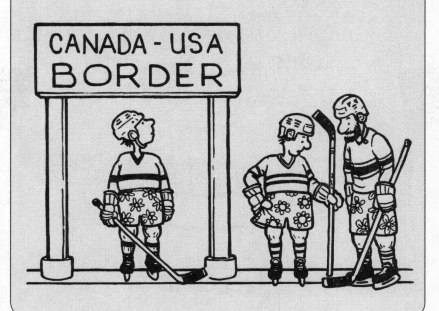

ON THE ROAD WITH STANLEY

The Stanley Cup spent a couple of days with Chicago Blackhawks players in Slovakia during the summer of 2010. During his time with the trophy, Marian Hossa ate perogies out of it. Tomas Kopecky enjoyed a Stanley Cup bowlful of traditional Slovakian soup.

VELCOME TO SLOVAKIA

When the Chicago Blackhawks won the Stanley Cup in 2015, Scotty Bowman was a senior advisor in the team's front office and got his name engraved on the trophy for the fourteenth time! In addition to his nine wins as coach and three as an advisor to the Blackhawks, Bowman also was a member of Detroit's front office when they won the Cup in 2008 and of Pittsburgh's when they won it in 1991. But he still hasn't beat out Jean Beliveau, who has his name on the Cup a record 17 times. Beliveau won it 10 times as a player in Montreal and seven more while working in the Canadiens' front office.

Coaching Records

Scotty Bowman holds the record for most Stanley Cup wins as a coach with nine. Bowman led Montreal to five titles, in 1973, 1976, 1977, 1978 and 1979. He later won the Cup as the head coach in Pittsburgh in 1992 and as coach of the Detroit Red Wings in 1997, 1998 and 2002. Bowman broke Toe Blake's record of eight Stanley Cups when Blake was the coach of the Montreal Canadiens between 1956 and 1968.

On May 7, 1985, Edmonton's Jari Kurri scored three goals in a 7–3 playoff win over Chicago. It was the first of three hat tricks Kurri got against the Black Hawks in the series. That's a record for the most hat tricks in one playoff series.

Twice in a Row

Mike Bossy was one of the greatest goal scorers in hockey history. Bossy scored 50 goals or more an amazing nine times in his 10-year career and had a total of 573 goals in just 752 regular-season games. Bossy was a pretty good scorer in the playoffs too! Not only did he lead the NHL in playoff goals three times, he scored the Stanley Cup–winning goal in 1982 and 1983.

Bossy is one of only two players in NHL history to score the Cup-winning goal in back-to-back years. The other one goes all the way back to the 1920s when Jack Darragh scored the Stanley Cup winner for the original Ottawa Senators in 1920 and 1921.

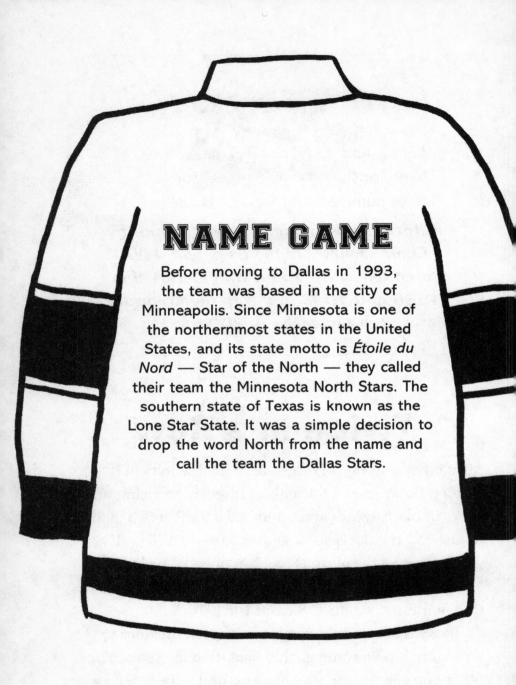

NAME GAME

Before moving to Dallas in 1993, the team was based in the city of Minneapolis. Since Minnesota is one of the northernmost states in the United States, and its state motto is *Étoile du Nord* — Star of the North — they called their team the Minnesota North Stars. The southern state of Texas is known as the Lone Star State. It was a simple decision to drop the word North from the name and call the team the Dallas Stars.

ON THE ROAD WITH STANLEY

Delivering the Stanley Cup to players and staff on that season's championship team makes for a busy summer of travel. Usually everything goes smoothly . . . but not always.

On August 23, 2004, the Hockey Hall of Fame employee who delivers the Cup got off a plane in the small town of Fort St. John in northern British Columbia. He was supposed to deliver the Stanley Cup to Jake Goertzen, head scout for the Tampa Bay Lightning.

He waited patiently for his special container to be unloaded from the luggage compartment. But the container never arrived. Turns out that the airplane had been full and the 16-kilogram (35 lb.) Stanley Cup had been removed because it was too heavy. It spent the night in the luggage area of the Vancouver airport, some 1,200 km (746 mi.) away. It arrived safely the next morning.

Edmonton On Ice

On November 22, 2003, the NHL staged its first outdoor hockey game. The "Heritage Classic" was held in Edmonton, Alberta. It was played on a rink built inside the city's football field, Commonwealth Stadium. At game time, the temperature in Edmonton was –18.6 degrees Celsius. That didn't stop diehard fans — the crowd that night swelled to 57,167, shattering the NHL attendance record at the time. They watched the Montreal Canadiens beat the Oilers 4–3.

While the Heritage Classic is usually held every few years and features Canadian teams and locations, the NHL's "Winter Classic" has become an annual New Year's tradition. Since 2008, outdoor games have been played in North American football and baseball stadiums. On January 1, 2014, a new record crowd of 105,491 saw the Toronto Maple Leafs defeat the Detroit Red Wings 3–2 in a shootout on a cold and snowy day at Michigan Stadium.

On the Move

After missing a whole season in 2004–05, more than 200 NHL players changed teams when the lockout ended. Every team in the NHL had new faces in training camp . . . except one. The San Jose Sharks did not add a single new player from outside their organization.

Rules to Live By

Even before the NHL lockout, many fans were complaining that games had become too boring. There was too much clutching and grabbing, and there wasn't enough scoring.

When the league came back in 2005–06, many rules were changed to try to open up the game. Goalies were forced to wear smaller equipment, and referees were told to call more penalties. Passing rules were also changed. Players could now pass the puck all the way from their own end up to the other team's blueline.

One of the biggest changes to the rules was the introduction of the shootout. If games are still tied after playing one overtime period, players now take penalty shots to decide the winner. Three players shoot for each team, but if the game is still tied after that, players keep shooting until there is a winner. The team that wins gets two points in the standings. The team that loses gets one.

Stanley's Namesake

A few weeks after Scotty Bowman coached the Canadiens to his first Stanley Cup victory in 1973, his wife gave birth to a baby boy. The Bowmans named their son Stanley . . . after the Stanley Cup. In 2010, Stan Bowman had his name engraved on the Cup as the general manager of the Chicago Blackhawks. By coincidence, the Blackhawks had been the team Montreal defeated back in 1973.

DID YOU KNOW?

The Canadiens' streak of five straight Cup wins from 1956 to 1960 came during a stretch where they reached the Finals for 10 straight seasons! Montreal made it every year from 1951 to 1960. In addition to their five wins in a row, the Canadiens also took home the Cup in 1953. Incredibly, they also won the Cup four years in a row from 1976 to 1979.

BY THE NUMBERS

NHL teams that have won the Stanley Cup two years in a row or more:

Team	Wins	Years
Montreal Canadiens	5	1956 to 1960
New York Islanders	4	1980 to 1983
Montreal Canadiens	4	1976 to 1979
Toronto Maple Leafs	3	1947 to 1949; 1962 to 1964
Pittsburgh Penguins	2	1991, 1992
Edmonton Oilers	2	1984, 1985; 1987, 1988
Philadelphia Flyers	2	1974, 1975
Detroit Red Wings	2	1936, 1937; 1954, 1955; 1997, 1998
Montreal Canadiens	2	1930, 1931; 1965, 1966; 1968, 1969
Ottawa Senators	2	1920, 1921

Ottawa Shoots to Victory

The NHL's first shootout occurred on the very first night of the 2005–06 season. After three periods of play, Ottawa and Toronto ended in a 2–2 tie. When overtime didn't decide it, the game went to a shootout.

Martin Havlat became the first player in NHL history to score a shootout goal, and Dany Heatley clinched the victory with another goal for Ottawa after Toronto was unable to score.

DID YOU KNOW?

On May 29, 1993, Wayne Gretzky scored a hat trick to lead Los Angeles to a 5–4 win over Toronto in Game 7 of the Western Conference Finals. It was Gretzky's eighth career playoff hat trick, breaking the record of seven he'd shared with Maurice Richard and Jari Kurri.

NAME GAME

The name Devils for New Jersey's hockey team was chosen from an old legend about a half-man, half-beast that roams the New Jersey countryside.

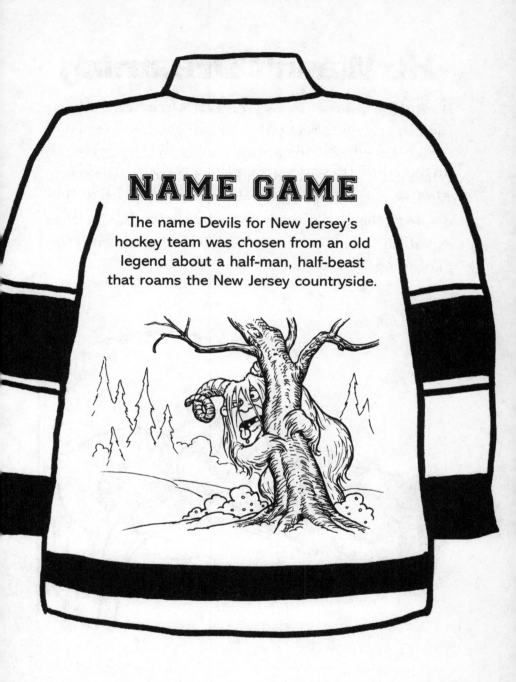

He Wasn't Dreaming

During the last few years of the 1970s, the New York
Islanders earned a reputation for being a great team in
the regular season that always choked in the playoffs.
When they finally won the Stanley Cup in 1980, Bryan
Trottier took it home with him . . . and slept with it! "I
wanted to wake up and find it right beside me," Trottier
explained. "I didn't want to think I'd just dreamed of this
happening."

Rockets Take Flight

Maurice "Rocket" Richard and his little brother Henri "Pocket Rocket" played together on the Canadiens team that won the Stanley Cup five years in a row. They were the last five years of Maurice's career and the first five years of Henri's.

The Richards, Henri (left) and Maurice (right) — teammates and brothers

ON THE ROAD WITH STANLEY

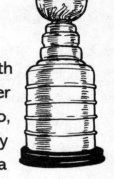

Patrick Kane had a busy day with the Stanley Cup during the summer of 2010. First, the native of Buffalo, New York, took the Cup to nearby Niagara Falls. Next, he took it to a cancer hospital in his hometown to cheer up the patients. Later, he had a party with some friends who all enjoyed eating chicken wings out of the Stanley Cup — Buffalo being the world's chicken wing capital. After that, Kane flew to Chicago where he and the Stanley Cup appeared onstage at a Jimmy Buffett concert.

The first American team to win the Stanley Cup was the Seattle Metropolitans of the PCHA. They beat the NHL champion Montreal Canadiens to win the Cup in 1917.

Flying Finn

Growing up in Finland in the 1970s, Jari Kurri didn't know much about the NHL. After playing for Finland at the 1980 Winter Olympics, Kurri was drafted by the Edmonton Oilers. During his first season in the NHL, Kurri was put on Wayne Gretzky's line. Cashing in on Gretzky's great passes, Kurri scored 32 goals as a rookie in 1980–81.

Gretzky and Kurri helped make Edmonton the greatest offensive team in NHL history. In 1981–82, the Oilers became the first team to score 400 goals in a season. By the 1983–84 season, they had upped their record to 446. The Oilers also won the Stanley Cup for the first time that season. Kurri scored 52 goals. He had 71 the next season and helped the Oilers repeat as Stanley Cup champions. In 1985–86, Kurri led the league with 68 goals.

Kurri helped the Oilers win the Stanley Cup again in 1987, 1988 and 1990. By the time he retired in 1998, Kurri had scored 601 goals and 1,398 points, making him the highest-scoring European player in NHL history at the time.

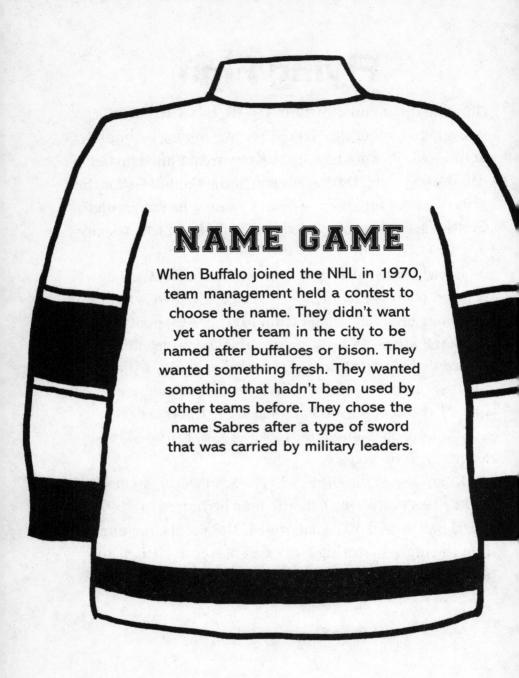

NAME GAME

When Buffalo joined the NHL in 1970, team management held a contest to choose the name. They didn't want yet another team in the city to be named after buffaloes or bison. They wanted something fresh. They wanted something that hadn't been used by other teams before. They chose the name Sabres after a type of sword that was carried by military leaders.

By George!

The award given to the NHL's best goalie is called the Vezina Trophy. It's named in honour of Georges Vezina, who was a star goalie with the Montreal Canadiens in the 1910s and '20s. Vezina joined the Canadiens for the 1910–11 season. For the next 15 years, he never missed a single game, regular season or playoffs. His streak got up to 367 games. Then, on November 28, 1925, Vezina missed a game due to a pain in his chest. It turned out the pain was caused by tuberculosis, a very serious lung disease. Sadly, he died four months later. In memory of him, the owners of the Canadiens presented the Vezina Trophy to the NHL for the 1926–27 season.

When Martin Brodeur was a boy in Montreal, Patrick Roy was his hero. On March 17, 2009, Brodeur broke his hero's NHL record for wins when he posted the 552nd victory of his career.

He Shoots,
He ... Soars?

The Boston Bruins had not won the Stanley Cup for 29 years. Then, in 1970, Bobby Orr won the series with an overtime goal. He lifted the puck past St. Louis goalie Glenn Hall just as Blues defenceman Noel Picard tripped him. Orr flew through the air with his arms raised in triumph and a big smile on his face. The picture of Orr celebrating his goal is one of the most famous images in hockey history.

Number four, Bobby Orr!

DID YOU KNOW?

The Vezina Trophy used to be awarded to the goalie (or goalies) on the team that allowed the fewest goals. The rules were changed for the 1981–82 season. That year, it was decided that the Vezina Trophy should go to the goalie who was voted to be the best in the league. A new trophy was donated to reward the goalies on the team that gives up the fewest goals. That trophy is the William Jennings Trophy. Jennings was president of the New York Rangers and helped popularize hockey in the United States.

BY THE NUMBERS

Here's a look at the goalies who have won the Vezina Trophy the most times:

Goalie	Wins
Jacques Plante	7
Dominik Hasek	6
Bill Durnan	6
Ken Dryden	5
Michel Larocque	4
Terry Sawchuk	4
Tiny Thompson	4
Martin Brodeur	4
Patrick Roy	3
Glenn Hall	3
George Hainsworth	3
Tony Esposito	3

George, the Sequel

After the death of Georges Vezina, George Hainsworth became the Montreal Canadiens' goaltender. And he was a good one! He won the Vezina Trophy the first three years it was presented. At that time, forward passing was not allowed in the offensive zone. Players trying to score could only shoot, stickhandle the puck or drop-pass it to someone, which gave goalies a big advantage.

During the 1928–29 season, Hainsworth set a record for shutouts that is not likely ever to be beaten. The season was just 44 games long that year, and he had 22 shutouts. He only let 43 shots get past him all season. His goals-against average was 0.92. The next year, the NHL changed its rules and allowed players to pass the puck forward from anywhere on the ice.

On February 6, 1973, Connie Madigan became the oldest rookie in NHL history when he played his first game for the St. Louis Blues. Madigan was 38 years old.

Farewell to the Forum

On March 11, 1996, the final game was played at the Montreal Forum. The Canadiens beat the Dallas Stars 4–1. The Forum had been the Canadiens' permanent home since 1926, and the final game there was a memorable moment for all hockey fans. The Canadiens won the game that night, as they had at the Forum more than 1,500 times. Winning was important, but it was the closing ceremonies that everyone would remember. The Canadiens had invited all of the team's living legends back to the Forum to give the building a proper farewell. Fans gave Maurice Richard, the greatest of all Canadiens, a standing ovation that lasted for nearly 10 minutes.

For many years, there has been a motto on the wall of the Canadiens' dressing room. It reads: "To you from failing hands we throw the torch; be yours to hold it high," and is from the poem "In Flanders Fields" by John McCrae. For the Canadiens, it means that each new generation of players is responsible for carrying on the team's great tradition. During the closing ceremonies, each of the team's former captains passed a flaming torch down a line. It was a fitting tribute for a team that had won the Stanley Cup 22 times while the Forum was their home. No NHL team has ever enjoyed so much success.

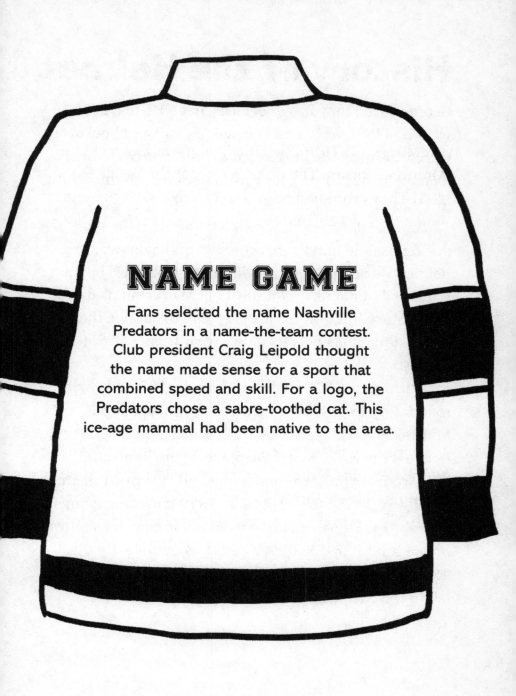

NAME GAME

Fans selected the name Nashville Predators in a name-the-team contest. Club president Craig Leipold thought the name made sense for a sport that combined speed and skill. For a logo, the Predators chose a sabre-toothed cat. This ice-age mammal had been native to the area.

History of the Helmet

George Owen may have been the first NHL player to wear a helmet. Owen had played football and hockey at Harvard University and is said to have worn a leather football helmet during his rookie season with the Bruins in 1928–29.

After Leafs forward Ace Bailey fractured his skull during a game in Boston, other Bruins began wearing helmets during the 1933–34 season. However, helmets remained unpopular. Not until Bill Masterton died of a head injury in 1968 did people begin to change their minds. Still, most players didn't wear them well into the 1970s.

During the 1970s, rules were passed to make helmets mandatory in junior leagues and the college ranks. Many of these players kept their helmets on when they reached the NHL. So did the players who joined the NHL from Europe, where they had always worn them. Finally, in 1979, the NHL passed a rule making helmets mandatory. However, anyone who had signed a contract before June 1, 1979, didn't have to wear one. By the 1995–96 season, Craig MacTavish was the last player left in the NHL who wasn't wearing a helmet.

CUP CHRONICLES

A third generation of the Patrick family has also been engraved on the Stanley Cup. Lynn Patrick's son Craig never won the Cup during his eight-year career as an NHL player, but he did get his name on the trophy as general manager of the Pittsburgh Penguins when they won it in 1991 and 1992.

Cherry and Grapes

With his loud suits and even louder opinions, Don Cherry has become one of the most famous people in hockey. Love him or hate him, people tune in to Coach's Corner on *Hockey Night in Canada* just to see what he has to say.

The Boston Bruins signed Don Cherry in 1952. He played hockey until 1972, but he only ever got to play one game in the NHL — a playoff game in 1955. He was a coach in the NHL from 1974 until 1980, mostly with the Bruins. He's been a TV commentator since then.

Cherry is known by the nickname "Grapes." Cherry actually got the nickname while playing minor league hockey with the Springfield Indians. Springfield owner Eddie Shore used to pay off the fines for players he liked, but he didn't like Cherry, so he wouldn't pay his fines. When Cherry got mad at another player and called him a name, Shore said, "Ah, that's just sour grapes," meaning that Cherry was just complaining. Soon, though, the rest of his teammates were calling him "Grapes" and the name stuck.

Maple Leaf Forever

Every year since 1965, the person who is voted the Most Valuable Player in the playoffs has received the Conn Smythe Trophy. This trophy was presented to the NHL in 1964 by the management of Maple Leaf Gardens. It honours Conn Smythe, a man who served as coach, manager, president, owner and governor of the Toronto Maple Leafs (sometimes all at the same time!) from 1927 to 1961. Smythe was also responsible for building Maple Leaf Gardens in 1931. That's why the Conn Smythe Trophy looks like Maple Leaf Gardens.

The first winner of the trophy, in 1965, was Jean Beliveau. He was the captain of the Maple Leafs' biggest rival, the Montreal Canadiens.

ON THE ROAD WITH STANLEY

During the summer of 2014, Kyle Clifford of the Los Angeles Kings used the Stanley Cup to take part in the ALS ice bucket charity challenge. Clifford filled the Stanley Cup bowl with ice water, which he then poured over the head of a young friend.

BY THE NUMBERS

Back in the 1950s and '60s, Terry Sawchuk set every important regular-season career record for goalies . . . including games played, seasons, wins and shutouts. It's taken many years, but all of Sawchuk's major records have now been broken. Here's a look at the NHL's top 10 shutout leaders:

Goalie	Seasons	Games	Shutouts
Martin Brodeur	22	1266	125
Terry Sawchuk	21	971	103
George Hainsworth	11	465	94
Glenn Hall	18	906	84
Jacques Plante	18	837	82
Alex Connell	12	417	81
Tiny Thompson	12	553	81
Dominik Hasek	16	735	81
Tony Esposito	16	886	76
Ed Belfour	17	963	76

In Memory

Maurice Richard was more than just a hockey hero. He was an idol to people all across Quebec when he starred with the Canadiens in the 1940s and '50s. When he died in Montreal on May 27, 2000, even people who had never seen him play were saddened.

To allow his fans to pay their last respects, Maurice Richard's body lay in state at the Molson Centre, the home rink of the Canadiens (now called the Bell Centre). More than 115,000 people filed past to say goodbye. On May 31, 2000, funeral services were held at the Notre-Dame Basilica, once the biggest church in North America.

After Jean Beliveau died on December 2, 2014, thousands of fans once again turned out at the Bell Centre to mourn the classy former Canadiens captain. The mayor of Montreal, the premier of Quebec, the prime minister of Canada and two former Canadian prime ministers all attended his funeral a few days later.

Years earlier, another Montreal hockey hero had been paid a similar tribute. Howie Morenz was the biggest star in hockey in the 1920s and '30s. On January 28, 1937, Morenz suffered a badly broken leg in an on-ice collision at the Montreal Forum. He died in hospital on March 8, 1937.

Morenz's funeral was held March 11 at centre ice in the Forum. About 12,000 people attended. Almost that many stood outside the building to pay tribute. Thousands more lined the streets en route to the cemetery in order to pay their last respects.

In 2009, Mario Lemieux won the Stanley Cup as the owner of the Pittsburgh Penguins. Back in 1991 and 1992, Lemieux had won the Cup as Pittsburgh's star player. Lemieux was the first person since Lester Patrick to win the Stanley Cup as both a player and as a team owner. The only other person in hockey history to have done that was Lester's brother — Frank Patrick. Frank was a player and the owner at the same time when the Vancouver Millionaires won the Stanley Cup in 1915.

True North . . . but Not So Strong

In the winter of 1904–05, a hockey team from Dawson City, Yukon, made the long voyage to Ottawa to challenge the Silver Seven for the Stanley Cup in a best-of-three series. The players left Dawson City to begin their trip to Ottawa on December 18, 1904. They had planned to travel by bicycle and by dogsled, but ended up walking most of the 530 km (329 mi.) to Whitehorse. It took them 10 days! From there, it was trains and boats the rest of the 6,000 km (3,728 mi.) to Ottawa, where they finally arrived on January 11, 1905, after several delays. The players had only one day of rest before starting the series on January 13. They lost that night 9–2. The next game on January 16, 1905, was even worse. Ottawa beat Dawson City 23–2.

The Zamboni Man

Zamboni is not just the name of the machine that cleans the ice at hockey games. It's the name of the man who invented it . . . Frank J. Zamboni.

Frank J. Zamboni was born on January 16, 1901, in Eureka, Utah. In 1920, he and his younger brother Lawrence went to California to work for their older brother George, who operated a garage in the twin cities of Hynes-Clearwater.

In 1927, Frank and Lawrence Zamboni built a factory that made blocks of ice. This ice was used in iceboxes, which were an early type of refrigerator.

By 1939, better brands of refrigerators meant that ice was in less demand. So, in 1940, Frank, Lawrence

The first Zamboni

and cousin Pete Zamboni opened a skating rink. At the time, resurfacing the ice in skating rinks meant pulling a scraper behind a tractor to shave the surface. Three or four workers would scoop away the shavings, spray water over the surface, squeegee it clean and allow the water to freeze. The whole process took more than an hour. Frank began to wonder how he could make a better sheet of ice in a shorter period of time. He started experimenting with a tractor in 1942, and by 1949, he had a design that he liked. Though he would continue to make improvements to his machine over the years, the Zamboni was born.

Then, in 1950, a famous figure skater, Sonja Henie, saw Frank's new machine. She ordered a Zamboni for her ice show in Chicago. In 1954, the Boston Bruins bought a Zamboni for the Boston Garden. Soon, every team in the NHL had a Zamboni for their arena. And they still do today.

Series of the Century

In the early days of hockey history, Canada was always the best at international competitions. Professional players were not allowed to compete at tournaments like the Olympics, but from the 1920s until the 1950s, Canada could send a top amateur team from anywhere in the country and expect to come home with a gold medal.

As the years went by, Canada's amateurs could no longer keep up. During the 1960s, the Soviet Union began to dominate. International games still did not allow NHL players, so Canada's best stars could never face the Soviets. Finally, arrangements were made for a special eight-game "Summit Series" in 1972. There would be four games in Canadian cities followed by four games in Moscow.

Most Canadians expected an easy victory for their NHL stars. They were stunned when the Soviets won the series opener in Montreal 7–3.

Team Canada won the second game in Toronto 4–1. Then, as there was no overtime in the series, there was a 4–4 tie in Winnipeg. Next came another loss, this time 5–3, in Vancouver. People all across the country were disappointed in their team. Many fans at the Vancouver game booed the Canadians.

When the series resumed in Moscow, the Soviets won again. Canada had been up 4–1 in the game, but lost 5–4. Now the Soviets led the series three games to one with one game tied. Canada would have to win all three remaining games to win the series. It seemed like an impossible feat, but they did it. In each game, Paul Henderson scored the winning goal. Game 8 was the most dramatic of all. Canada was trailing 5–3 after two periods. Early in the third, Phil Esposito scored to make it 5–4. Midway through the period, he set up Yvan Cournoyer with the tying goal. Then, with just 34 seconds left in the game, Henderson scored again. Canada had won the series!

After more than forty years, the series is still remembered as the most dramatic of all time.

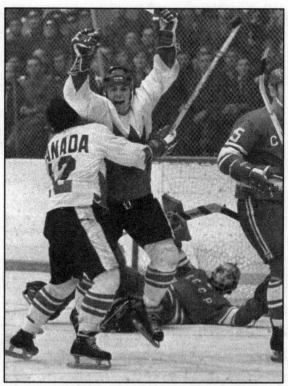

Henderson celebrates his game-winning goal.

Good As Gold

After 1972, more and more professional players were allowed to play at international tournaments. Still, it wasn't until 1998 that active NHL players could compete at the Winter Olympics. When the Canadian men's team won the gold medal at Salt Lake City in 2002, it marked the first time in 50 years that Canada had won the Olympic gold medal in hockey. In fact, Canadian hockey players won two gold medals in 2002. The women's team also won the Olympic Championship that year and followed it with another gold medal at the 2006 Winter Olympics. The Canadian men's and women's teams once again swept the gold medals in Olympic hockey in 2010 in Vancouver and in 2014 in Sochi, Russia.

On June 4, 1996, the Stanley Cup Finals opened with the Colorado Avalanche defeating the Florida Panthers 3–1 in Denver. This was the first time in NHL history that both teams in the Finals had never played for the Stanley Cup.

Cancelled Cup

When the NHL lockout cancelled the 2004–05 hockey season, it marked just the second time since 1893 that a hockey season had ended without a Stanley Cup champion. The only other time was in 1919. During 1918 and 1919, a very serious flu epidemic, commonly referred to as the Spanish Flu, spread around the world. Millions of people died.

In March 1919, the Montreal Canadiens were facing the Seattle Metropolitans in the Stanley Cup Finals. It was a gruelling series, with two long overtime games. As the series stretched on, several Canadiens players got sick. The final game of the series was scheduled for April 1, but so many players were suffering from the flu that the game had to be cancelled. There would be no Stanley Cup champion for 1919.

Sadly, Canadiens star Joe Hall was so sick that he died on April 5, 1919. Canadiens owner George Kennedy never fully recovered from his bout with the flu. He died in October 1920.

ON THE ROAD WITH STANLEY

When New Jersey Devils goalie Martin Brodeur was a boy in Montreal, he and his friends used to play road hockey and pretend that they were playing for the Stanley Cup. So when Brodeur won the Cup for the first time in 1995, he got all his old buddies together for a road hockey tournament. The winners got to carry the Stanley Cup around in triumph! Brodeur's team lost that day, so when he won the Cup again in 2000, he organized a rematch. This time, his team won.

Brodeur and his friends got to break their tie in 2003 when the Devils won the Stanley Cup for the third time. Not only was the Cup on the line that year, but so was Brodeur's 2002 Olympic gold medal. The tournament went right down to the wire, with Brodeur's team winning the final game 7–5. Brodeur's four children had a good time with the Stanley Cup that day too. In the morning, they ate their breakfast cereal out of the bowl. At night they used it to hold the marshmallows they roasted in their backyard firepit.

One-Eyed Wonder

Frank McGee was the star of the Ottawa Silver Seven. He had lost the sight in one eye due to an injury early in his career, but it barely slowed him down. In 1905, McGee scored 14 goals in Ottawa's 23–2 win over Dawson City to set a Stanley Cup record that will likely never be broken!

Surprise Attack

When teams pulled their goalies during the 1930s, they always did it during a stop in play. But New York Rangers coach Frank Boucher thought it would give him an advantage if he pulled his goalie while play was going on. He tried it for the first time on January 14, 1940. The Rangers had gone 19 games in a row without a loss. They were going for number 20, but they were losing to Chicago 2–1.

At the end of the second period, Boucher told goalie Dave Kerr that if the Rangers were still trailing by one late in the game he was going to pull him. Boucher told him he wasn't going to wait for a stop and that Kerr should watch for a signal. Boucher gave Kerr the signal with about 1:30 remaining in the game. The move certainly caught everyone by surprise, but it didn't work. The Rangers lost. Their streak was over, but hockey had a brand-new tactic.

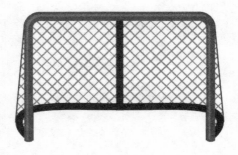

The Golden Goal

Having already won 13 gold medals at the 2010
Vancouver Olympics, Canada had tied the record for the
most first place finishes at a single Winter Games. It was
an amazing achievement, but there was one gold medal
that many Canadians were still dreaming about: the gold
in men's hockey. The deciding game was played on the
final day of the Olympics, and breaking the record with
the gold medal in hockey would be the perfect ending.

Team Canada hadn't been doing as well on home ice
as people expected. In the opening round, they needed
overtime to beat Switzerland and lost their game against
the United States. Canada woke up with an easy 8–2
win against Germany to qualify for the playoffs, and
then defeated Russia 7–3 in the quarter-finals. Facing
Slovakia in the semifinals, Team Canada held on for a
3–2 victory after nearly letting a 3–0 lead slip away. The
gold medal game was a rematch against the Americans.
Canada was leading 2–1, but the U.S. tied it up with just
25 seconds remaining. Although Sidney Crosby was
Canada's biggest star, he hadn't played his best hockey
during the Olympics. Still, Crosby was there when it
mattered most. He scored the gold medal–winning goal
at 7:40 of overtime to set off a celebration all across the
country.

Divide and Conquer

As the NHL has grown from three teams to 30 since its first season in 1917–18, the league has often shuffled its divisions. From the 2000–01 to 2012–13 seasons, the NHL's 30 teams were split into six divisions of five teams apiece, playing in two different conferences. Starting in 2013–14, the league switched to a new format. There are still two conferences (the Eastern Conference and the Western Conference), but there are now just four divisions. The Eastern Conference is made up of the Atlantic Division and the Metropolitan Division, with eight teams in each. The two divisions in the Western Conference are the Central Division and the Pacific Division. Each of those divisions has only seven teams. Still, all NHL teams play 82 games apiece, and eight teams from each conference make the playoffs, even though the Eastern Conference has more teams.

Pick a Puck

Everyone knows that real hockey pucks are made of rubber. But if you're only playing hockey for fun, almost anything will do. Plastic pucks can be used for floor hockey; tennis balls work well for road hockey; even a tin of tuna works if you're playing on a frozen lake! But sometimes, people just have to get creative. This was especially true in hockey's early days. Back then a lump of coal may have been used as a puck. But it wasn't always the best idea, since it was pretty valuable and tended to break apart. A small bit of a sawed-off tree branch was better and cheaper. But there was another source of pucks that was absolutely free. Believe it or not, when horses used to pull carts on city streets, people often used their frozen plops of manure as hockey pucks. Yuck!

Howe About That!

Every time the Detroit Red Wings have won the Stanley
Cup, someone named Howe has gotten his name engraved
on the trophy. Syd Howe was a member of the Red Wings
when they won the Stanley Cup their first three times
back in 1936, 1937 and 1943. Syd was a great player, but
no relation to the greatest Red Wing of all time, Gordie
Howe. Gordie won the Cup four times with Detroit: 1950,
1952, 1954 and 1955. It took 42 years for the Red Wings
to win the Cup again, but when they did win it in 1997
and 1998, Gordie's son Mark Howe (who had been a pretty
great player himself!) was a member of the team's scouting
staff. Mark Howe was on the Red Wings' staff for their
Stanley Cup wins in the 2000s too.

The Howes: Mark, Gordie and Marty

Coffey Talk

Paul Coffey may have been the best skater in hockey history. He was blazing fast and super smooth.

Coffey worked hard to become a great skater, but a lot of his skill was just natural-born talent. He did have one trick though. He used to wear skates that were too small. He once joked to a reporter that he wanted to fool his feet into thinking that the faster they skated, the faster the game would end and he could take the skates off.

Coffey's blazing speed made him a perfect fit with Wayne Gretzky and the high-flying Edmonton Oilers. He joined the team in 1980, and was soon being compared to Bobby Orr. During the 1983–84 season, Coffey joined Orr as just the second defenceman in NHL history to score 40 goals in a single season. Two years later, Coffey nearly became the only defenceman in history to score 50 goals in one season. He wound up with 48, breaking Orr's old record of 46.

Even after he left the Oilers, Coffey was often among the league's leaders in assists. When he retired in 2001, his lifetime total of 1,135 assists ranked fourth in NHL history.

Fast Starters

Each year dozens of players make their debut in the NHL, although most of them see only limited action. Every so often, though, a rookie has such a spectacular season that it's obvious he's destined to become a real superstar. The 2005–06 season was unusual in that the NHL saw two incredible rookie performances.

Sidney Crosby was just 17 years old when he was chosen first overall by the Pittsburgh Penguins in the 2005 NHL Entry Draft. Two months after turning 18, he started his NHL career, getting two assists in his first two games. Then, in just his third game, he scored his first goal. It was a pretty good start to the season, and to his NHL career.

By the end of the 2005–06 season, Crosby had scored 39 goals and added 61 assists for a total of 102 points. He was the youngest player in NHL history to score 100 points in a season, and was just the seventh rookie in NHL history to do it. Still, Crosby wasn't even the top-scoring rookie in the NHL that season! That title belonged to Alexander Ovechkin, who also started off his NHL career with a bang.

Like Crosby, Ovechkin was also a number-one pick in the NHL Entry Draft — the Washington Capitals selected him first overall in 2004. Though he is two years older than Crosby, Ovechkin also made his NHL debut on October 5, 2005, due to the 2004–05 lockout. He didn't just score one goal in his very first game, he scored two!

Ovechkin's rookie season was even more spectacular than Crosby's. His 52 goals made him just the fourth rookie in NHL history to score 50 or more, and his 54 assists gave him 106 points.

Not bad for a couple of rookies!

Votes for Women

In December 2007, the International Ice Hockey Federation (IIHF) announced that three women had been voted into the IIHF Hall of Fame for the first time in its history. Angela James and Geraldine Heaney of Canada and Cammi Granato of the United States were officially inducted at a ceremony in May 2008.

James and Granato became the first female members of the Hockey Hall of Fame in Toronto in 2010. Heaney joined them there in 2013.

Lucky Number

Sidney Crosby wears number 87 because of his birthday, which is August 7. That's the eighth month and the seventh day. And what year was he born? 1987, of course.

ON THE ROAD WITH STANLEY

Doug Weight celebrated his sweet Stanley Cup victory with the Carolina Hurricanes in 2006 with a giant ice cream sundae. Weight, his wife and their three kids filled the bowl of the Cup with gallons of ice cream, chocolate sauce, M&Ms and chocolate chips. Mmmmm.

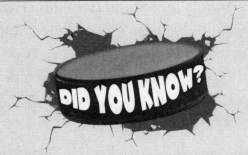

Dan Cleary became the first player from Newfoundland to win the Stanley Cup when he won it as a member of the Detroit Red Wings in 2008. Cleary was born in Carbonear, Newfoundland, on December 18, 1978, and began his NHL career with the Chicago Blackhawks in 1997.

Keepers of the Cup

Like many VIPs, the Stanley Cup doesn't travel alone.
Whenever the Cup has to be somewhere — whether
it's a charity event, an arena appearance or part of
the summer victory tour — someone from the Hockey
Hall of Fame goes with it. Together, the Stanley Cup's
"bodyguards" are known as the Keepers of the Cup.

ON THE ROAD WITH STANLEY

Luc Robitaille was a member of the Detroit Red Wings when he finally won the Stanley Cup in 2002. For most of his career, Robitaille had starred with the Los Angeles Kings, so when he got to spend a day with the Stanley Cup, he brought it to Los Angeles. Robitaille loaded family and friends onto a rented bus, and they all took the Cup on a tour of the city. His favourite stop was taking the Stanley Cup up to the famous Hollywood sign on the hillside above the city.

A Family Affair

Athletic skill seems to run in Alex Ovechkin's family. His father Mikhail was a professional soccer player in Russia. His mother Tatiana won Olympic gold medals in women's basketball in 1976 and 1980.

An Oldie but a Goodie

Fifty goals in a single season has long been a milestone in hockey. Most of the greatest scorers in NHL history have managed to top the 50-goal mark, but sometimes it takes a player a long time to get there. The NHL's oldest 50-goal scorer is John Bucyk. He was 35 years old when he scored 51 goals for the Boston Bruins in 1970–71. Teemu Selanne just missed breaking that record when he scored 48 goals in 2006–07 at the age of 36.

BY THE NUMBERS

Here's a look at the seven NHL rookies
who have scored 100 points or more:

Player	Team
Teemu Selanne	Winnipeg Jets
Peter Stastny	Quebec Nordiques
Alex Ovechkin	Washington Capitals
Dale Hawerchuk	Winnipeg Jets
Joe Juneau	Boston Bruins
Sidney Crosby	Pittsburgh Penguins
Mario Lemieux	Pittsburgh Penguins

Year	Goals	Assists	Points
1992–93	76	56	132
1980–81	39	70	109
2005–06	52	54	106
1981–82	45	58	103
1992–93	32	70	102
2005–06	39	63	102
1984–85	43	57	100

In an NHL shootout, the home team always has the choice of whether it wants to shoot first or second.

Six of a Kind

The biggest hockey family in NHL history is the Sutter family of Viking, Alberta. Six Sutter brothers played in the NHL, including twin brothers Rich and Ron. The other Sutter brothers to play were Brent, Brian, Darryl and Duane.

Growing up on a farm in Alberta, the Sutters all pushed each other in everything they did, especially hockey. They weren't the most talented players, but they worked hard. Gary was the oldest of the boys, and the best according to his six brothers, but he left hockey early to help run the farm. Gary watched as Brian led the way to the NHL, paving a path for their five other siblings.

Brian, the eldest of the six Sutters who played in the NHL, was drafted by the St. Louis Blues in 1976 and began his NHL career the following year.

In terms of statistics, Brent was the most successful of the Sutter brothers. He played in 1,111 games and scored 363 goals. If you measure success by Stanley Cup wins, then Duane was the best. He won the Cup four times in a row with the New York Islanders in the early 1980s. Brother Brent played alongside him on two of those teams.

A new generation of Sutters has now begun to make its way into the NHL. Brent's son Brandon, Darryl's son Brett and Duane's son Brody have upped the family total to nine players.

BY THE NUMBERS

Here's a look at the NHL records for most goals in a Stanley Cup game:

Most Goals, Both Teams, One Game

15   Chicago Black Hawks (8) at Montreal
      Canadiens (7) in Game 5, May 8, 1973.
      (Montreal won series 4–2.)

Most Goals, One Team, One Game

9   Detroit Red Wings in Game 2,
      April 7, 1936.
      (Toronto 4 at Detroit 9. Detroit won
      series 3–1.)

      Toronto Maple Leafs in Game 5,
      April 14, 1942.
      (Detroit 3 at Toronto 9. Toronto won
      series 4–3.)

Most Goals, One Player, One Game

4   Newsy Lalonde, Montreal, in Game 2, March 22, 1919. Montreal 4 at Seattle 2.

Babe Dye, Toronto, in Game 5, March 28, 1922. Vancouver 1 at Toronto 5.

Ted Lindsay, Detroit, in Game 2, April 5,1955. Montreal 1 at Detroit 7.

Maurice Richard, Montreal, in Game 1, April 6, 1957. Boston 1 at Montreal 5.

Willie O'Ree became the first black player in NHL history when he played two games with the Boston Bruins in January of 1958. He also played 43 games with the Bruins during the 1960–61 season. Though his NHL career was brief, O'Ree had a very long career in professional hockey. It stretched from 1955 to 1979. From 1961–62 to 1973–74, O'Ree was one of the best — and most popular — players in the Western Hockey League, a top minor league. Almost nobody knew it during his playing days, but something made Willie O'Ree's career even more remarkable: he was almost completely blind in one eye. A puck struck O'Ree in his right eye during a game in the 1955–56 season. He lost 95 percent of his vision in that eye, and doctors told him he would never play hockey again. Proving them wrong, he returned to action just eight weeks later. Long after his playing career, Willie O'Ree was named Director of Youth Development for the NHL/U.S.A. Hockey Diversity Task Force in 1998.

Willie O'Ree on the ice during a pre-game warm-up with his Boston Bruins teammates

His First Wasn't First

Patrick Kane was the first player selected in the 2007 NHL Entry Draft. He played his first NHL game with the Chicago Blackhawks just a few months after that, on October 4, 2007, and he scored his first goal in his second game two days later . . . Or did he?

Kane scored the only goal in a shootout to give Chicago a 4–3 win over the Detroit Red Wings on October 6, 2007. However, goals scored in a shootout don't count as official goals in NHL statistics. So, even though he won the game for Chicago that night, Kane wasn't actually credited with scoring a goal! His first official goal came nearly two weeks later when he scored against the Colorado Avalanche on October 19.

On March 14, 1948, Montreal's Maurice Richard scored a hat trick with three unassisted goals. The next player to match this feat was Rick Nash when he was with the Columbus Blue Jackets — 61 years later on March 7, 2009.

ON THE ROAD WITH STANLEY

In February 2000, the Stanley Cup attended the Native Hockey Tournament at Rankin Inlet, Nunavut. The temperature was about −65 degrees Celsius! Still, some people drove nearly 400 km (249 mi.) on snowmobiles just to see the Cup. While it was there, the Cup toured the town and even made a brief stop inside an igloo.

Wanna Bet?

The Quebec Bulldogs of the National Hockey Association won the Stanley Cup in 1912 and 1913. Few people had seen their success coming. Even some members of the team didn't think they would win it in 1912. When the Bulldogs did win, two of their own players had to pay up on some pretty strange bets. Goldie Prodger had to wheel a teammate around town in a wheelbarrow, while Joe Hall had to stickhandle a peanut an entire city block . . . using only a toothpick!

DID YOU KNOW?

Swedish superstar Nicklas Lidstrom became the first European-born player to captain his team to a Stanley Cup Championship when the Detroit Red Wings beat the Pittsburgh Penguins in 2008. This was his second "first": when Detroit won the Cup back in 2002, Lidstrom was the first European player to win the Conn Smythe Trophy as the playoffs' most valuable player.

Rules and Records

Wayne Gretzky holds a lot of NHL records, but because of some league rules, there are a couple he hasn't been able to lay claim to.

Gretzky had an incredible start to his NHL career. His totals of 51 goals, 86 assists and 137 points would have been rookie records, had he qualified. Why didn't he? The NHL didn't consider Gretzky to be a rookie because he had spent the year before playing in the World Hockey Association (WHA). He also didn't win the Calder Memorial Trophy, which goes to the rookie of the year.

Another league rule kept Gretzky from being the youngest player in history to win the Art Ross Trophy as the NHL scoring leader. Gretzky's 137 points in 1979–80 actually tied him for the league lead with NHL veteran Marcel Dionne. But because of a league rule that says if there's a tie for points in the Art Ross race, the trophy goes to the player who has scored the most goals that season, Dionne won it. He had 53 goals; Gretzky had 51.

Gretzky won the Art Ross Trophy the following year, when he was 20. Sidney Crosby was 19 when he won the Art Ross Trophy in 2006–07, making him the youngest person in NHL history to win it.

When Wayne Gretzky started playing hockey, he wore number 9 in honour of Gordie Howe, his favourite player. He didn't start wearing 99 until he played junior hockey with the Sault Ste. Marie Greyhounds. Another player already had 9, so Gretzky had to choose another one. He tried 14 and 19 before finally settling on 99.

DID YOU KNOW?

The NHL scoring race has ended in a tie two other times. Bobby Hull and Andy Bathgate both had 84 points in 1961–62. Hull won the Art Ross Trophy that year because he had 50 goals and Bathgate had only 28. Jaromir Jagr and Eric Lindros were tied for the league lead with 70 points in 1994–95. Jagr won the Art Ross Trophy that year because he had 32 goals and Lindros had 29.

Captain Kid: Part II

When the Pittsburgh Penguins named Sidney Crosby their captain on May 31, 2007, he became the youngest captain in NHL history. Crosby was 19 years and nine months old, beating Vincent Lecavalier's previous record by two months. The pressure didn't seem to bother Crosby at all. In 2009, he led the Penguins to win the Stanley Cup.

On September 4, 2012, the Colorado Avalanche announced that Gabriel Landeskog would be their new captain. He was just 19 years and 286 days old, which made him 11 days younger than Crosby was when he became Pittsburgh's captain.

The Youngest Kid

The youngest person ever to play for a Stanley Cup champion was Larry Hillman. Hillman was just 18 years, two months and nine days old when the Detroit Red Wings won the Cup in 1955.

Other 99s

Early in Wayne Gretzky's career, two other NHL players wore number 99. Wilf Paiement wore it for the Toronto Maple Leafs from 1979 to 1982, and Rick Dudley wore 99 for the Winnipeg Jets in 1980–81. Way back in 1934–35, three different players — Leo Bourgeault, Desse Roche and Joe Lamb — wore 99 for the Montreal Canadiens, all in the same season!

Fast Tricks

The fastest hat trick in NHL history was scored in just 21 seconds. Bill Mosienko of the Chicago Black Hawks got three goals against the New York Rangers at 6:09, 6:20 and 6:30 of the third period on March 23, 1952. Mosienko's hat trick helped the Black Hawks rally to a 7–6 victory.

Almost 55 years later, on February 19, 2007, Ryan Malone of the Pittsburgh Penguins got his own unique kind of fast hat trick. Malone scored each of his three goals during the first minute of play in each period. He scored 45 seconds into the first period, 49 seconds into the second and 48 seconds into the third.

On October 18, 2008, Pittsburgh's Sidney Crosby and Evgeni Malkin both reached milestones on the same play: Crosby scored his 100th career goal and Malkin got an assist for his 200th career point. Crosby asked for the puck to be split in half so they could each have a souvenir.

Do Canadians love hockey? You can take it to the bank! Or, at least, you could. From 2002 to 2013, all the five-dollar bills printed in Canada had a picture on the back of children sledding, skating and playing hockey. There was also a quotation from Roch Carrier's well-known short story, The Hockey Sweater.

Your Name Here

Rules for how many names are engraved on the Stanley Cup have changed over the years. In the early days, when teams had fewer players and staff, there wasn't much of a problem. These days, however, every championship team submits a list to the NHL commissioner for approval of the names they would like to include. A total of 53 names can be engraved. Every player who played at least one game in the Finals is assured of getting his name on the Stanley Cup. So is every player who played in at least half the team's games during the regular season . . . provided he was still on the roster at the end of the year. Players who don't meet these requirements can still be included on the Cup if they are judged to have made a significant contribution to the team. Most teams also engrave the names of as many coaches and front-office personnel on the Stanley Cup as they have room for.

The NHL changed its rule about minor penalties before the 1956–57 season. Until then, two-minute penalties lasted the full two minutes no matter how many goals were scored. The new rule allowed the penalized player to return to the ice if the team gave up a power-play goal. The reason for the rule? The Montreal Canadiens' power play was just too good! Take a look at the November 5, 1955, game between the Boston Bruins and the Montreal Canadiens: Montreal's Jean Beliveau scored three goals against the Boston Bruins in just 44 seconds while the Canadiens had a man advantage. Ouch!

Rocketing to the Top

In 2006–07, Vincent Lecavalier became the first French-Canadian player to win the Maurice "Rocket" Richard Trophy, which was donated to the NHL by the Montreal Canadiens in 1999. The trophy is awarded each year to the player who leads the NHL in goals scored. Richard was a star player with the Canadiens from 1942 to 1960 and is a legendary hero in Quebec.

Vincent Lecavalier receiving the Maurice Richard Trophy with The Rocket's brother Henri

CUP CHRONICLES

Mark Messier is the only player in NHL history to captain two different Stanley Cup–winning teams. Messier was captain of the Edmonton Oilers when they won the Stanley Cup in 1990 and was also captain of the New York Rangers when they won in 1994.

You Say It's Your Birthday

Players like Sidney Crosby, Vincent Lecavalier, Patrick Kane and Wayne Gretzky are among many who have made it to the NHL at the age of 18. But can you imagine a hockey player making it to the NHL before he'd celebrated five birthdays? How about making the Hall of Fame before his 11th birthday? Impossible? Well, it's happened . . . sort of.

Henri Richard was born on February 29, 1936 — a leap day. Technically, his birthday comes around only once every four years. So when Maurice Richard's little brother reached the NHL in 1955, he'd only had four actual birthdays . . . even though he was really 19 years old. Henri Richard was 43 years old when he was inducted into the Hall of Fame in 1979 . . . but he wouldn't actually have his 11th birthday until one year later.

BY THE NUMBERS

Red Kelly won the Stanley Cup four times with the Detroit Red Wings in the 1950s and another four times with the Toronto Maple Leafs in the 1960s. He's the only person on the list of players with the most Stanley Cup championships who didn't win any of his with the Montreal Canadiens. Here's the list of players with the most Cup wins:

Player	Cups
Henri Richard	11
Jean Beliveau	10
Yvan Cournoyer	10
Claude Provost	9
Red Kelly	8
Maurice Richard	8
Jacques Lemaire	8
Serge Savard	8
Jean-Guy Talbot	7

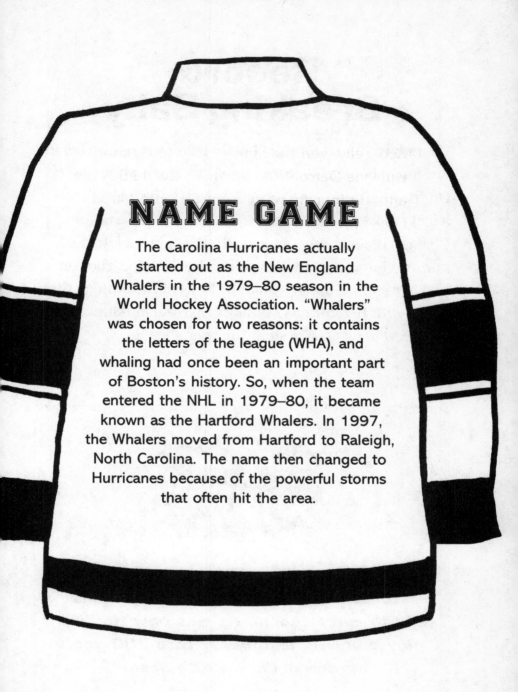

NAME GAME

The Carolina Hurricanes actually started out as the New England Whalers in the 1979–80 season in the World Hockey Association. "Whalers" was chosen for two reasons: it contains the letters of the league (WHA), and whaling had once been an important part of Boston's history. So, when the team entered the NHL in 1979–80, it became known as the Hartford Whalers. In 1997, the Whalers moved from Hartford to Raleigh, North Carolina. The name then changed to Hurricanes because of the powerful storms that often hit the area.

Record-Breaking Baby

There have been stories of babies being in the Cup before, but how about when they were just over an hour old? On the afternoon of October 12, 2010, the wife of Dave Knickerbocker, an executive in the front office of the Chicago Blackhawks, gave birth to a baby girl. Just 97 minutes later, the newborn Elena Ruth Knickerbocker had her picture taken inside the bowl of the Stanley Cup, along with her father's Stanley Cup ring, making her the youngest baby ever to sit in the cherished bowl.

On February 5, 2009, Alex Ovechkin scored his 200th NHL goal in just his 296th career game. He was only the fifth player in NHL history to score 200 goals in fewer than 300 games.

Baby in a Bowl

The first known picture of a baby sitting in the bowl of the Stanley Cup is of the son of Georges Vezina, the great Montreal Canadiens goalie. Joseph Louis Marcel Vezina was born the night after the Canadiens won their first Stanley Cup title in 1916. He later became better known as Marcel Stanley Vezina.

Dryden's Debut

Hall of Fame goalie Ken Dryden is the only player in NHL history to win a major individual trophy before winning the Calder Trophy as rookie of the year. Dryden was called up to the Montreal Canadiens late in the 1970–71 season. He won all six games he played and was given the starting job for Montreal in the playoffs. Dryden's spectacular performance in the post-season helped the Canadiens win the Stanley Cup and earned him the Conn Smythe Trophy as the most valuable player in the playoffs. A year later, Dryden won the Calder Trophy after spending his first full season in the NHL.

Worth the Wait

Raymond Bourque was one of the greatest defencemen in NHL history. In fact, he is the all-time scoring leader among NHL blueliners. He also won the Norris Trophy as best defenceman five times. Yet as good as he was, Raymond Bourque played 21 seasons in the NHL without winning the Stanley Cup. He finally won it in season number 22, with the Colorado Avalanche, in 2001. Counting the regular season and playoffs, it took Bourque 1,826 games to win the Stanley Cup . . . and he won it in the last game he ever played. No one else in hockey history has ever had to wait so long to be a champion.

DID YOU KNOW?

The first time that Stanley Cup games were broadcast on television was in 1953 between the Montreal Canadiens and the Boston Bruins. The Canadiens won the series four games to one.

On June 13, 1974, Don Cherry was named coach of the Boston Bruins. As a player, Cherry spent 16 years in the minor leagues and played only one game in the NHL. As a coach, he led Boston to four division titles in his five seasons. He won the Jack Adams Award as coach of the year in 1975–76, but never won the Stanley Cup.

ON THE ROAD WITH STANLEY

On February 2, 2007, the Stanley Cup champion Carolina Hurricanes were welcomed to the White House in Washington by American president George W. Bush. The very next day, the Stanley Cup visited Canada's Governor General Michaelle Jean for a special reception at Rideau Hall in Ottawa.

DID YOU KNOW?

Fred Sasakamoose is recognized as the first Indigenous person to play in the NHL. He played 11 games with the Chicago Black Hawks in 1953–54, making his debut at Maple Leaf Gardens in Toronto on February 27, 1954. A Cree, Sasakamoose was born on the Sandy Lake Reserve in Saskatchewan on December 25, 1933. He was inducted into the Saskatchewan Sports Hall of Fame in 2007. However, some believe that Sasakamoose may not really have been the first. Paul Jacobs, a Mohawk from Kahnawake, Quebec, went to training camp with the Toronto Arenas in 1918, but it's unclear if he ever actually played in a game. Others believe that Bud Maracle, who played 11 games for the New York Rangers in 1930–31, may also have been an Indigenous person. It's even possible that the old Springfield Indians minor league hockey team got their name because Maracle was one of the team's original players.

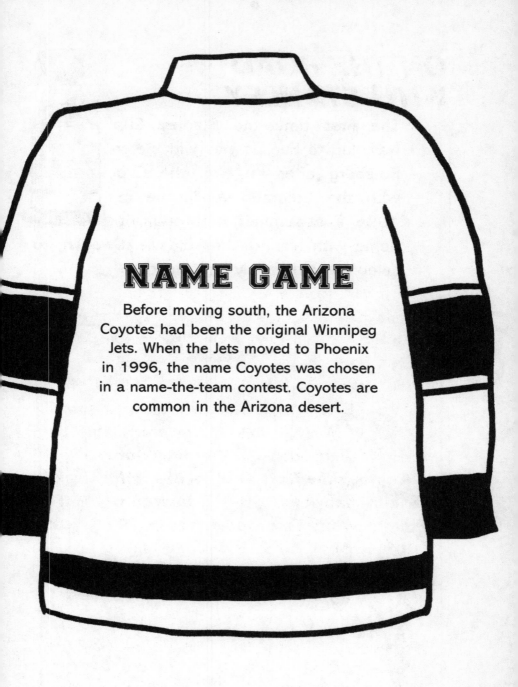

NAME GAME

Before moving south, the Arizona Coyotes had been the original Winnipeg Jets. When the Jets moved to Phoenix in 1996, the name Coyotes was chosen in a name-the-team contest. Coyotes are common in the Arizona desert.

ON THE ROAD WITH STANLEY

The first time the Stanley Cup travelled to Europe was with Peter Forsberg after he won the Cup with the Colorado Avalanche in 1996. That summer, he brought it home with him to Ornskoldsvik, Sweden, to celebrate with family and friends.

Going Home

In recent years, the Stanley Cup has travelled all over Europe with players from countries such as Sweden, Russia, Slovakia, the Czech Republic and Germany. But a trip to England in April of 2006 marked the first time the Stanley Cup had ever gone home.

Phil Pritchard of the Hockey Hall of Fame took the Stanley Cup to London to meet Edward Stanley, the great-great grandson of Lord Stanley, who had donated the trophy back in 1892 when he was Governor General of Canada. The Cup also visited the site of the silversmith shop where the original bowl was purchased.

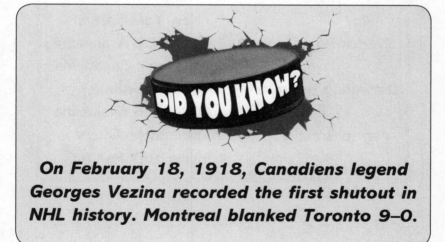

On February 18, 1918, Canadiens legend Georges Vezina recorded the first shutout in NHL history. Montreal blanked Toronto 9–0.

BY THE NUMBERS

Only six players in NHL history have had their numbers retired by two different teams.

Player	Number	Teams Retired
Gordie Howe	9	Detroit Red Wings Hartford Whalers/ Carolina Hurricanes
Bobby Hull	9	Chicago Blackhawks Winnipeg Jets/ Arizona Coyotes
Mark Messier	11	Edmonton Oilers New York Rangers
Patrick Roy	33	Colorado Avalanche Montreal Canadiens
Raymond Bourque	77	Boston Bruins Colorado Avalanche
Wayne Gretzky	99	Edmonton Oilers New York Rangers

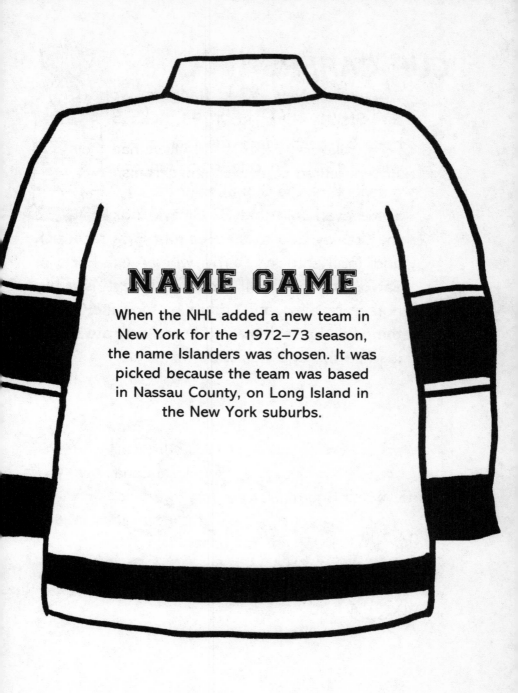

NAME GAME

When the NHL added a new team in New York for the 1972–73 season, the name Islanders was chosen. It was picked because the team was based in Nassau County, on Long Island in the New York suburbs.

CUP CAPERS

When the New York Rangers won the Stanley Cup in 1994, it had been 54 years since the team's last win in 1940. To celebrate, Rangers players took the Cup all over the city. Some even said that Ed Olczyk took the Stanley Cup to the Belmont Park racetrack and let Kentucky Derby winner Go For Gin eat out of the bowl! Although Olczyk is a big horseracing fan, and admits he took the Cup to the track, he says that no horse ever ate out of it while the Cup was with him.

DID YOU KNOW?

When rookie Guillaume Latendresse wore 84 for the Montreal Canadiens in 2006–07, it meant that at some point in history a player in an NHL game had worn every number from 0 and 00 to 99.

First to 500

With a goal on October 19, 1957, Maurice "Rocket" Richard of the Montreal Canadiens became the first player in NHL history to score 500 career goals. When Richard retired a few years later, he had scored 544 goals. Today, Wayne Gretzky holds the NHL career record with 894 goals. Still, the 500-goal plateau is considered a major milestone for any player who reaches it.

ON THE ROAD WITH STANLEY

Cristobal Huet is just the third player from France (after Philippe Bozon and Sebastien Bordeleau) to play in the NHL. As the backup goalie for the Chicago Blackhawks in 2009–10, he was the first French Stanley Cup champion. Huet brought the Stanley Cup to France for the first time that summer, visiting his hometown of Grenoble and then taking it to Paris for pictures at the Eiffel Tower.

The Cup with Cristobal Huet in Paris

CUP CHRONICLES

Alberta teams dominated the Stanley Cup during the 1980s. From 1983 until 1990, either the Calgary Flames or the Edmonton Oilers made it to the Finals every season. Between them, they won the Stanley Cup six times.

Chris Pronger was the first player to score a goal on a penalty shot during the Stanley Cup Finals. Pronger was playing for the Edmonton Oilers, and he beat Carolina Hurricanes goalie Cam Ward in Game 1 of the Stanley Cup Finals on June 5, 2006. Unfortunately for Oilers fans, the Hurricanes won 5–4 that night and went on to take the series in seven games.

Three of a Kind

Before he reached the NHL, future Hall of Famer Denis
Savard was already part of a famous line with the
Montreal Junior Canadiens. Savard centred Denis Cyr
and Denis Tremblay on a line known as "Les Trois
Denis." Not only were all three players named Denis,
they had all been born on the same day — February 4,
1961 — and they all grew up within three blocks of
each other in the Montreal suburb of Verdun!

Young Gun

Jordan Staal was the youngest player in the NHL during his rookie season of 2006–07. He turned 18 only a few weeks before the season began. On October 21, 2006, he became the youngest player in NHL history to score a goal on a penalty shot. On February 10, 2007, he became the youngest player ever to score a hat trick.

Empty Cup

In the spring of 2006, the Carolina Hurricanes beat the Edmonton Oilers to win the Stanley Cup. One year later, neither team even made it to the playoffs! That marked the first time since the NHL took control of the Cup in 1926–27 that both finalists from the year before failed to make the playoffs the next season.

One Is the Loneliest Number

Until the 1960s, every NHL team only had one goalie on its roster. In the early days, if a goalie got hurt in a game, play was delayed until he could be patched up. If the goalie was hurt too badly to continue, his team would actually have to put another player in net!

In 1950, the NHL passed a new rule that said every home team had to have a spare goalie at each game. This goalie would take over for either team in case of an injury or illness. These so-called "house goalies" were usually the team trainer, or a local amateur star. The most famous house goalie was Ross "Lefty" Wilson. Wilson was a former minor league goalie who served as the Detroit Red Wings' assistant trainer and often went in net during practice. Three times between 1953 and 1957, Wilson had to take over in net during games played at the Detroit Olympia. In all, Wilson played a total of 85 minutes and only allowed one goal!

Number Four, Bobby Orr

Bobby Orr wore number 4 when he starred with the Boston Bruins in the 1960s and '70s. His name and the number just seem to go together — maybe because they rhyme! But Orr was given a different number when he first joined the Bruins. He wore 30 when he got to his first training camp, and wore 27 in exhibition games. At the time, Albert "Junior" Langois wore 4 for Boston. When Langois got injured, then sent to the minors, Orr asked if he could have Langois's number. Orr had worn 2 when he played junior hockey, but Boston had retired that number in honour of another great defenceman, Eddie Shore. The Bruins had also retired 3, so Orr figured 4 was as close as he could get!

Doing It the Hard Way

Seven players in NHL history have entered the 500-goal club by scoring a hat trick to reach the milestone. The first was Jean Beliveau in 1971. The others are Wayne Gretzky, Mario Lemieux, Mark Messier, Brett Hull, Jaromir Jagr and Mats Sundin.

Early Adventures in Ottawa

According to legend, after the Ottawa Silver Seven won the Stanley Cup in 1905, a few of the players wondered if anyone could kick it across the Rideau Canal. The Cup was punted football-style, but didn't make it all the way and landed in the middle of the canal. Fortunately, the water was frozen, so it didn't sink.

Whistle While You Work

When the Toronto Wellingtons travelled to play the Winnipeg Victorias for the Stanley Cup in 1902, John Ross Robertson, the president of the Ontario Hockey Association, came up with a clever new way of letting Toronto hockey fans know how their team had done. Robertson arranged for the Toronto Railway to use the giant steam whistle on top of its powerhouse as a signal during the series. After the final results were received by telegraph, the whistle would blow twice if the Wellingtons had won, but there would be a third whistle if the winner was Winnipeg. "Many a house had somebody listening for the hoarse blasts," reported the *Globe* newspaper in Toronto, "and many a one held his breath after two were sounded, hoping there would be no third."

Unfortunately for Toronto fans, there was a third whistle after both games. The Winnipeg Victorias won each one 5–3 to sweep the best-of-three series in two straight games.

Lanny McDonald was a longtime NHL star who finally won the Stanley Cup for the first time in the last game he ever played. McDonald had scored 66 goals for the Calgary Flames back in 1982–83. He was a sixteen-year veteran by 1988–89 and co-captain of the team, but his best days were well behind him. Despite growing a bushy red beard for luck to go with his trademark shaggy moustache, McDonald hadn't scored a single goal during the 1989 playoffs. He was even benched for three games during the Stanley Cup Finals against Montreal, but he returned to the lineup for Game 6. Early in the second period, McDonald finally scored. His goal put Calgary in front 2–1 and sparked the Flames to a 4–2 victory. McDonald had saved his best for last.

They Don't Ask How, Just How Many

It wasn't pretty when Jeremy Roenick scored his 500th career goal for the San Jose Sharks on November 10, 2007. Roenick dumped the puck into the Phoenix Coyotes' end from outside the blueline. The puck hit the glass behind the net, bounced off the goal, deflected off goalie Alex Auld's skate, twirled toward the goal line and then skittered in off of Auld's stick. "I wish for his sake it could have been nicer," Auld said.

DID YOU KNOW?

Lanny McDonald is the only player in NHL history to score exactly 500 goals during his career. The Calgary Flames star scored his 500th goal, got his 1,000th point and won the Stanley Cup for the first time all in his final NHL season of 1988–89.

The Champion of Champions

Henri Richard has more Stanley Cup rings than fingers! Richard played on more Stanley Cup–winning teams than any player in hockey history. He played with the Montreal Canadiens for 20 seasons (1955–56 to 1974–75) and won the Stanley Cup 11 times. Jean Beliveau nearly matched Richard's record, playing on 10 Stanley Cup–winning teams during his 20 seasons in Montreal.

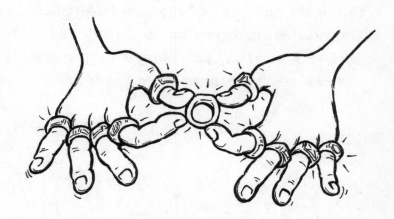

DID YOU KNOW?

The tradition of naming three stars at a hockey game began after Imperial Oil introduced "3 Star" gasoline at Esso stations back in 1931. By 1932, the company was placing ads in newspapers choosing the three stars of hockey and football games. When Imperial Oil became the main sponsor of Hockey Night in Canada radio broadcasts during the 1936–37 season, choosing the game's three stars became very popular.

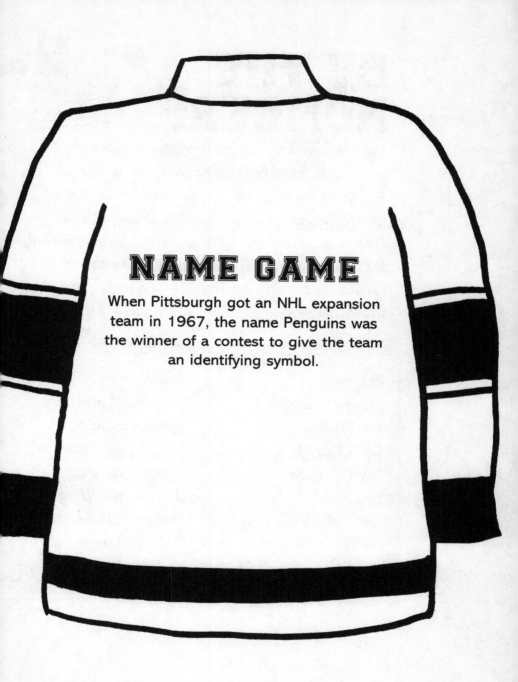

NAME GAME

When Pittsburgh got an NHL expansion team in 1967, the name Penguins was the winner of a contest to give the team an identifying symbol.

BY THE NUMBERS

Joe Malone was one of the greatest goal scorers in early hockey history. On January 31, 1920, Malone scored seven goals in a single game! That's an NHL record that still stands. Over the years, seven different players (including Joe Malone himself) have come close to the record by scoring six goals in a game. Here are those players:

Player	Team
Newsy Lalonde	Montreal Canadiens
Joe Malone	Quebec Bulldogs
Corb Denneny	Toronto St. Pats
*Cy Denneny	Ottawa Senators
Syd Howe	Detroit Red Wings
Red Berenson	St. Louis Blues
Darryl Sittler	Toronto Maple Leafs

*Corb Denneny and Cy Denneny were brothers.

Date

January 10, 1920

March 10, 1920

January 26, 1921

March 7, 1921

February 3, 1944

November 7, 1968

February 7, 1976

DID YOU KNOW?

In 1964, an injury to goalie Terry Sawchuk forced the Detroit Red Wings to use minor leaguer Bob Champoux in a playoff game. Even though the Red Wings won 5–4, the NHL decided this wasn't a fair way to do things. A new rule was introduced stating that every team would have to have two goalies dressed for playoff games in 1965. Then, before the start of the 1965–66 season, the rule was expanded to state that every team had to have two goalies in their lineup for every single NHL game.

That's Gotta Hurt!

When Bobby Hull starred in the 1960s, he had the hardest shot in the NHL. He may even have had the hardest shot of all time: measuring devices weren't as accurate then, but it was said he could shoot the puck 193 kilometres (120 miles) per hour!

Going in Goal

The first player to take over in goal during an NHL game was a defenceman named Harry Mummery. In a game against the Ottawa Senators on February 4, 1920, Quebec Bulldogs goalie Frank Brophy was struck by a hard shot right over his heart. There were only two minutes left in the second period, but Brophy couldn't continue, so veteran Mummery took over and stayed in net for the rest of the game. He was bombarded with more than 30 shots but only let in three. Still, Ottawa beat Quebec 5–0. Later in the season, Quebec used Mummery in goal again for two full games, both of which were also against the Senators. On March 8, Mummery was beaten for 11 goals in an 11–4 loss, but just two days later, Mummery and the Bulldogs beat Ottawa 10–4.

Mummery made one final appearance as a goalie during the 1921–22 season, once again against Ottawa. But this time Mummery was playing for the Hamilton Tigers. Hamilton goalie Howard Lockhart was hit in the face by a shot (goalies didn't wear masks at the time) near the end of the first period. It was 4–1 for Ottawa when Mummery took over, but he allowed the Senators just two more goals and Hamilton rallied to win 7–6 in overtime.

Think They Needed a Rest?

The NHL record for most goals in a single period is nine. The Buffalo Sabres scored nine times against the Toronto Maple Leafs in the second period of a game on March 19, 1981. The final score that night was 14–4.

Gretzky's Little Brother

Wayne Gretzky has a brother who also played in the NHL. Brent Gretzky played in 10 games for the Tampa Bay Lightning in 1993–94. He played in three games with Tampa the following year before being sent back to the minors. Brent Gretzky scored just one goal in his NHL career.

Where'd the Puck Go?

The Stanley Cup series between the Ottawa Silver Seven and Rat Portage Thistles in March 1903 was played during unusually warm weather that left the playing surface in terrible shape. At one point during the first game of the series, the puck fell through a hole in the ice and disappeared!

BY THE NUMBERS

Clint Benedict holds the career record for shutouts in Stanley Cup games. Benedict recorded eight shutouts during the five Stanley Cup series he played with the Ottawa Senators and Montreal Maroons in the 1920s. Benedict is also one of only three goalies to post three shutouts in a single Stanley Cup Final. Here's a look at the complete list:

Year	Player
1926	Clint Benedict, Montreal Maroons 3 shutouts in 4 games
1945	Frank McCool, Toronto Maple Leafs 3 shutouts in 7 games
2003	Martin Brodeur, New Jersey Devils 3 shutouts in 7 games

Like Father, Like Son

Bobby Hull and Brett Hull are the only father-son combination in hockey history to have both scored over 500 goals in their careers. Bobby scored 610 goals in his NHL career; Brett scored 741.

ON THE ROAD WITH STANLEY

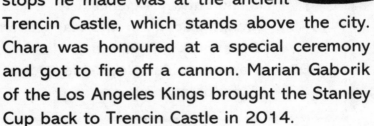

When Boston Bruins captain Zdeno Chara brought the Stanley Cup to his hometown of Trencin, Slovakia, in the summer of 2011, one of the stops he made was at the ancient Trencin Castle, which stands above the city. Chara was honoured at a special ceremony and got to fire off a cannon. Marian Gaborik of the Los Angeles Kings brought the Stanley Cup back to Trencin Castle in 2014.

Howe Could He Compete?

When it comes to NHL families, Gordie Howe is most famous for playing alongside his two sons, Mark and Marty. But did you know that Gordie Howe also had a brother who played in the NHL? Vic Howe didn't do quite as well as his older sibling. He played for the New York Rangers, but he only played in 33 games during parts of three seasons in the 1950s. Gordie Howe scored 801 goals in his NHL career; Vic Howe only scored 3.

That One Was Easy

Four of hockey's greatest goal scorers scored their 500th career goal into an empty net: Mike Bossy, Wayne Gretzky, Jari Kurri and Keith Tkachuk.

Goals and Saves

Toronto Maple Leafs star Charlie Conacher was the NHL's top goal scorer five times in six seasons between 1930–31 and 1935–36. But his talents weren't limited to just scoring: Conacher was pretty good at preventing goals too! He took over in net four times in his career when his goalie was either injured or penalized. He played a total of 10 minutes in the net during his career and never gave up a single goal.

Bobby's Brother

Bobby Hull not only had a star hockey player for a son, he had a brother who was pretty good too. Dennis Hull played in the NHL for 14 seasons from 1964 to 1978. He and Bobby were teammates with the Chicago Black Hawks for eight seasons. Dennis scored 40 goals in his best season in 1970–71, and had 303 in his career. Combined with Bobby's 610 goals, that gives the Hulls 913. No two brothers in NHL history have ever scored more.

Classy Cassie

On October 14, 2006, Cassie Campbell became the first woman to do colour commentary on a *Hockey Night in Canada* broadcast. A year later, in the fall of 2007, she became the first women's hockey player to be inducted into Canada's Sports Hall of Fame. Cassie Campbell retired as a player in 2006 after playing as a top forward and captaining the Canadian Olympic women's hockey team in 2002 and 2006.

Cassie Campbell behind the *Hockey Night in Canada* desk

The Night the Lights Went Out

The Boston Bruins were down three games to nothing to the Edmonton Oilers in the 1988 Stanley Cup Finals, but they were fighting to stay alive on home ice in Game 4. They were leading until late in the second period when Craig Simpson scored for the Oilers to tie the game at 3–3. A split second later, the lights went out in the Boston Garden. It was a massive power failure, and the game had to be suspended. All the players' statistics still counted, but the game itself did not. The series resumed in Edmonton two nights later. When the Oilers won it, they were credited with a four-game sweep.

DID YOU KNOW?

On February 25, 1990, Brett Hull of the St. Louis Blues scored his 59th goal of the 1989–90 season (then scored two more). Brett broke his family's NHL record. His father, Bobby Hull, had scored 58 goals for Chicago in 1968–69.

Half a Goal?

During the second game of the 1902 Stanley Cup
series between the Winnipeg Victorias and the Toronto
Wellingtons, there was a scramble around the Winnipeg
net and the puck broke into two pieces. Winnipeg goalie
Art Brown figured the play would be stopped, but it
wasn't. Toronto's Chummy Hill scooped up half of the
puck and shot it into the net. The referee ruled it a goal,
and Toronto went ahead 2–1 . . . but went on to lose the
game and the series.

A few years later, a referee ruled a play no goal when
a player scored with a broken puck. He said that the rules
stated that a puck was supposed to be one-inch thick, and
if something that was smaller than that went into the net,
it wasn't really a puck, so it shouldn't count as a goal.
Ever since then, hockey rules have said that the whole
puck has to go across the goal line for a goal to count.

A Good Year

You often hear about players "drinking from the Cup."
The tradition was started back in 1896 after the Winnipeg
Victorias beat the Montreal Victorias and celebrated by
drinking champagne out of the Stanley Cup bowl. When
they got back to Winnipeg with the trophy, their fans
gave them the first Stanley Cup parade. Both of these are
traditions that carry on to this day.

Maurice Richard, Gordie Howe and Bobby Hull all famously wore number 9 on their sweaters. However, none of them started off with that number. Richard actually wore 15 when he joined the Montreal Canadiens, but asked to switch to 9 when his first child was born and weighed 9 lb. (4 kg). Howe wore 17 when he first joined the Detroit Red Wings, but asked to switch to 9 after he figured out that players with lower numbers got better seats when the team travelled by train. Hull wore 16, then 7, before he finally settled on 9.

CUP CHRONICLES

Did King Clancy really play all six positions in one Stanley Cup game? Stories say he did it with the Ottawa Senators on March 31, 1923. Clancy was normally a defenceman, but he definitely spent two minutes between the pipes when Ottawa goalie Clint Benedict was penalized for slashing in that game. However, it was likely an earlier playoff game where Clancy faced off as a centre, played both sides of the defence and skated up and down both wings too.

DID YOU KNOW?

On March 18, 1930, rookie Paul Thompson of the Chicago Black Hawks fired a shot past Boston Bruins goalie Cecil "Tiny" Thompson. This was the first time in NHL history that a player scored a goal against his brother. Tiny got the last laugh, however, as his Bruins blasted Paul's Black Hawks 9–2.

Penalties Too

Injuries weren't the only reason players sometimes had to take over in goal. In the early days of the NHL, goalies actually had to serve their own penalties. When a goalie was sent to the penalty box, his team had to scramble to find a player to replace him. In those days a minor penalty lasted a full two minutes, even if a team scored a power-play goal, so a penalty to a goalie could mean real trouble.

A game between the Boston Bruins and the Toronto Maple Leafs on March 15, 1932, is a perfect example of how bad things could get for a team if they lost their goalie to a penalty. Maple Leafs goalie Lorne Chabot was called for tripping early in the first period. The Leafs tried using three different defencemen in the net, but the Bruins scored a goal against each one of them! Boston went on to win the game 6–2.

Where'd the Cup Go?

With his Philadelphia Flyers trailing
the Edmonton Oilers three games
to one in the 1987 Stanley Cup
Finals, Flyers coach Mike Keenan
came up with a pretty good way to
motivate his players. Before the next
game, Keenan brought the Stanley
Cup into the Flyers dressing room.
The Flyers went out and won the
game 4–3. Before the next game,
Keenan brought the Cup into the dressing room again,
and the Flyers won. Keenan wanted to keep his new
ritual going, but when the Flyers returned to Edmonton
for Game 7, he was told that the Cup had been delayed in
shipping and wasn't there yet. Edmonton went on to win
the game and take the series. It was later revealed that
the Cup really had been there all along but that Oilers
assistant trainer Sparky Kulchisky had hidden it so that
the Flyers couldn't have it!

BY THE NUMBERS

Wayne Gretzky set an all-time record with 10 assists in the 1988 Stanley Cup Finals. He also scored three goals to set another record with 13 points. Here's a look at the NHL's leading scorers in a single Stanley Cup series:

Points	Player
13	Wayne Gretzky, Edmonton Oilers, 1988 (3G–10A in 4 games plus suspended game)
12	Gordie Howe, Detroit Red Wings, 1955 (5G–7A in 7 games)
	Yvan Cournoyer, Montreal Canadiens, 1973 (6G–6A in 6 games)
	Jacques Lemaire, Montreal Canadiens, 1973 (3G–9A in 6 games)
	Mario Lemieux, Pittsburgh Penguins, 1991 (5G–7A in 5 games)
	Daniel Briere, Philadelphia Flyers, 2010 (3G–9A in 6 games)

Lester to the Rescue

The most famous case of a non-goalie guarding the net in an NHL game came during the 1928 Stanley Cup Finals. But it wasn't a player who took over this time: it was the coach.

The New York Rangers had already lost the first game to the Montreal Maroons. Now, midway through the second period of the game, it was scoreless. Then a shot struck the Rangers' goalie, Lorne Chabot, directly on his left eye. He couldn't continue and was sent to the hospital.

The Rangers had no spare goalie. Alec Connell of the Ottawa Senators was at the game in Montreal that night, so the Rangers asked for permission to borrow him. The Maroons said no. The players insisted that the Rangers had to follow the rules about using someone who was already on their team. Coach Lester Patrick chose himself.

Patrick had once been a star defenceman. He'd played a full season as recently as 1925–26, and he had played 10 minutes in goal back in 1921–22. Still, he was now 44 years old. Could he possibly hold back the Maroons' powerful attack?

With the Rangers playing tight defence in front of him, Patrick stopped every shot he faced but one. The Rangers managed one goal themselves, so the game went into overtime. Then, at 7:05 of the extra session, the Rangers scored again. Even the Maroons fans stood and cheered as Lester led the Rangers off the ice.

After the game the Maroons agreed to let the Rangers use Joe Miller of the New York Americans for the rest of the series. Following a 2–0 loss to the Maroons in Game 3, Miller posted a shutout of his own in Game 4 to push the best-of-five series to the limit. Miller was cut and suffered two black eyes in Game 5, but he hung on for a 2–1 victory that gave the Rangers the Stanley Cup.

DID YOU KNOW?

Before he was a coach, Lester Patrick had been a star player. He also made a few emergency appearances in goal back then too. He even made a brief appearance in an early Stanley Cup game. Late in the first game of their series in Ottawa in 1904, Brandon goalie Dugald Morrison got a penalty. Lester Patrick filled in for him and stopped the only shot he faced.

Made to Measure

In the earliest days of hockey, goalies didn't wear much more protection than any other player. Then, in the early 1890s, goalies began wearing cricket pads on their legs. The pads helped to ease the pain from hard shots, but since they wrapped so closely around a goalie's legs, the puck sometimes would deflect off them and keep on going right into the net.

Starting in the 1920s, special pads — much wider than cricket pads — were made especially for hockey goalies. In order to make sure that goalies didn't wear pads that were so wide they blocked too much of the net, the NHL passed a rule before the 1925–26 season that said goalie pads could not be more than 12 in. (30 cm) wide. Over the years, the rule flip-flopped between 12 in., 10 in. (25 cm) and 12 in. again. Then another change was made following the 2004–2005 lockout, when the NHL introduced several new rules in order to bring more scoring back into the game. Now goalie pads cannot be more than 11 in. (28 cm) wide.

Seventh Heaven

The first time that a best-of-seven Stanley Cup series was played was in 1939, when the Boston Bruins beat the Toronto Maple Leafs in five games. Two years later, Boston became the first team to sweep a seven-game series when they beat the Detroit Red Wings four in a row. Just two years after that, Toronto's win over Detroit marked the first time a series went the full seven games.

On October 14, 1979, Wayne Gretzky scored his first NHL goal. It was a power-play goal with 69 seconds left in the game to give Edmonton a 4–4 tie with Vancouver. Gretzky actually fanned on his backhand shot, but the puck dribbled between the legs of goalie Glen Hanlon.

Photo Opportunities

After their victory in 1988, Wayne Gretzky gathered his Edmonton Oilers teammates together on the ice for a picture with the Stanley Cup. Since then, every winning team has celebrated their victory by posing for an on-ice photo.

Wayne Gretzky in the first Stanley Cup–winning team photo

Unmasked Man

Jacques Plante is known as the man who popularized the goalie mask. Plante wore a mask for the first time during the 1959–60 season and helped the Canadiens win the Stanley Cup that year. Even so, goalie masks didn't catch on right away. The last goalie to play for the Stanley Cup without wearing a mask was Montreal's Rogatien Vachon in 1969.

Pop's Pads

Emil (Pop) Kenesky made harnesses for horses in Hamilton, Ontario. By 1917, he had opened his own business. But Pop was also a hockey fan. While watching local church league games in the early 1920s, he noticed the way shots sometimes bounced into the net right off a goalie's cricket pads, and he didn't like it. Using the tools of his harness-making trade, Pop began making improvements to the pads the local goalies were wearing.

Percy Thompson was the owner of the Hamilton Tigers NHL team. In 1924, he asked Pop to repair the pads of Tigers goalie Jake Forbes. The Tigers had always been a bad team, but once Forbes started wearing his new Kenesky pads, the team started to win. Soon, other NHL goalies were asking Pop to make pads for them too.

Pop Kenesky's pads were made of leather and stuffed with deer hair and kapok (a silky fibre made from the seeds of tropical plants). All the pads were handmade, so it took a long time to make them. He could never make very many at a time, but all the best goalies in hockey wanted to use Kenesky pads. So Pop just kept on making them. He put in a full eight hours a day at his store until he was 86 years old.

Kenesky pads remained very popular in the NHL right up until the 1990s. By then, new materials had become available. Pads could now be made much more quickly, and they were much lighter and stayed drier too. There is still a Kenesky Sports store in Hamilton, and it still sells goalie equipment, but the store is no longer owned by the Kenesky family and it no longer makes its own brand of equipment.

Of all the fathers and sons who have played in the NHL, Bobby Hull and Brett Hull are the only ones who have both won the Hart Trophy as league MVP. Bobby won the Hart Trophy in 1965 and 1966. Brett won it 1991.

All Hail Hayley

In December 2007, Hayley Wickenheiser became the first hockey player ever to be named Canada's female athlete of the year. Wickenheiser took over from Cassie Campbell as captain of the National Women's Hockey Team in 2007 and led Canada in reclaiming the World Championship from the United States. She had eight goals and six assists in five games at the tournament and was named the most valuable player.

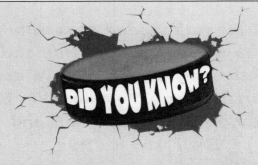

Wayne Gretzky, Jari Kurri and Glenn Anderson are the only three teammates to each score 50 goals in the same season, and they did it twice! All three topped 50 with the Edmonton Oilers in 1983–84 and 1985–86.

NAME GAME

San Jose joined the NHL for the 1991–92 season. Like many team names, the name Sharks was picked out of 5,000 entries in a name-the-team contest. There are many shark research facilities in the San Francisco Bay area in California, where San Jose is located.

Comeback Kids

In the first round of the 2014–15 playoffs, the Los Angeles Kings dropped their first three games to the San Jose Sharks. The Kings stormed back to win four games in a row and take the series. Then the Kings won their next three series to win the Stanley Cup for the second time in three years. Los Angeles was just the fourth team in NHL history to rally from a three-games-to-nothing deficit to win a playoff series. In 2010, Philadelphia beat the Boston Bruins in the second round after losing the first three games. The New York Islanders also did it back in 1975. The first team to bounce back from being down three games to nothing was the Toronto Maple Leafs, who did it against Detroit in the Stanley Cup Finals in 1942.

Overtime and Again

Of the 16 wins it took the Montreal Canadiens to earn the Stanley Cup in 1993, a record 10 came in overtime. In fact, after dropping the first game of the playoffs in overtime that year, the Canadiens won 10 straight in extra time, including three in the Finals.

Back-to-Back Bernie

The Philadelphia Flyers were known as the "Broad Street Bullies" when they won the Stanley Cup in 1974 and 1975. They were tough, and took plenty of penalties to intimidate their opponents. The team had lots of talent, too, with future Hall of Famers like Bobby Clarke, Bill Barber and Bernie Parent. Parent won the Conn Smythe Trophy both years the Flyers won the Cup, making him the first player to be named playoff MVP in back-to-back years. The only other back-to-back winner is Mario Lemieux with the Pittsburgh Penguins in 1991 and 1992.

Billy Smith of the New York Islanders was the first goalie in NHL history to be credited with a goal. It happened on November 28, 1979. Smith didn't really score though. He was simply the last Islander to touch the puck before a Colorado Rockies player accidentally shot it into his own net.

Last of His Kind

On October 16, 1960, Jerry Toppazzini of the Boston Bruins became the last position player to play goal in an NHL game. At the time, no player had been forced to replace a goalie since 1941. But Boston goalie Don Simmons was cut under the eye by a shot from Chicago Black Hawks' Eric Nesterenko with less than 30 seconds remaining in the game. Rather than wait for the Black Hawks' house goalie to suit up, Toppazzini went in the net instead. He didn't face any shots as the final few seconds wound down.

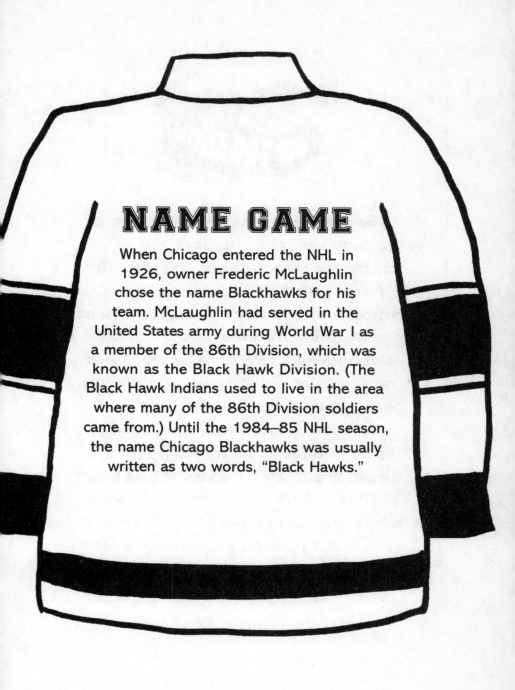

NAME GAME

When Chicago entered the NHL in 1926, owner Frederic McLaughlin chose the name Blackhawks for his team. McLaughlin had served in the United States army during World War I as a member of the 86th Division, which was known as the Black Hawk Division. (The Black Hawk Indians used to live in the area where many of the 86th Division soldiers came from.) Until the 1984–85 NHL season, the name Chicago Blackhawks was usually written as two words, "Black Hawks."

DID YOU KNOW?

The first goalie to actually score a goal by shooting the puck the length of the ice into an open net was Ron Hextall of the Philadelphia Flyers. Hextall scored after the Boston Bruins pulled their goalie in a game on December 8, 1987. To prove it was no fluke, he did it again in a playoff game against the Washington Capitals two years later. Since then, several other goalies have scored goals too. Some, like Hextall, have shot the puck in, but others, like Billy Smith, were simply the last player on their team to touch the puck before someone else scored in their own net.

CUP CHRONICLES

Hal Winkler's name appears on the Stanley Cup with the 1929 Boston Bruins even though he didn't play a single minute with the team that season! Winkler had starred for Boston in 1927–28, but was in the minors in 1928–29. Still, his name got engraved on the Stanley Cup as the Bruins' "sub-goaltender."

Thanks for Coming

Goalie Robbie Irons was just expecting to sit on the bench when he was called up to the St. Louis Blues for a game on November 13, 1968. After all, the Blues had two future Hall of Fame goaltenders on their roster: Jacques Plante was out with a groin injury, but that still left Glenn Hall to play. Unfortunately for the Blues, Hall got into an argument with the referee just two minutes after the opening faceoff that night and was given a game misconduct.

Blues coach Scotty Bowman didn't think that Irons was ready to play. He told his rookie goalie to stall for time while Plante came down from the stands to suit up. But the referee wasn't buying Irons's stall tactics. Faced with a two-minute delay-of-game penalty, Bowman sent Irons into the net. By 5:01 of the first period, Plante was ready. Irons had played just three minutes (and faced no shots), but his moment in the spotlight was over. He played 12 more years in the minor leagues, but never got another chance in the NHL.

On March 31, 1994, Christian Soucy played three minutes in goal for the Chicago Blackhawks. It was the only NHL appearance of his career, so Soucy and Robbie Irons are considered tied for the shortest careers in NHL history. However, Soucy actually played three minutes and 21 seconds, while Irons only played three minutes and one second.

Bep Was Just a Boy

The youngest player in NHL history was Armand "Bep" Guidolin. Bep Guidolin was just 16 years old when he joined the Boston Bruins in 1942–43. With so many older hockey players serving in the military during World War II, many young players got an early chance to play in the NHL.

DID YOU KNOW?

The Boston Bruins posted a record of 38–5–1 during a 44-game season in 1929–30. In today's 82-game NHL, that would equal a record of 70–10–2 and 144 points! The Bruins never lost two games in a row during the entire season . . . until they reached the Stanley Cup Finals. Then the Montreal Canadiens swept Boston for two straight wins in a best-of-three series. After that, the NHL expanded the Finals to a best-of-five series. The current best-of-seven playoff format was introduced in 1939.

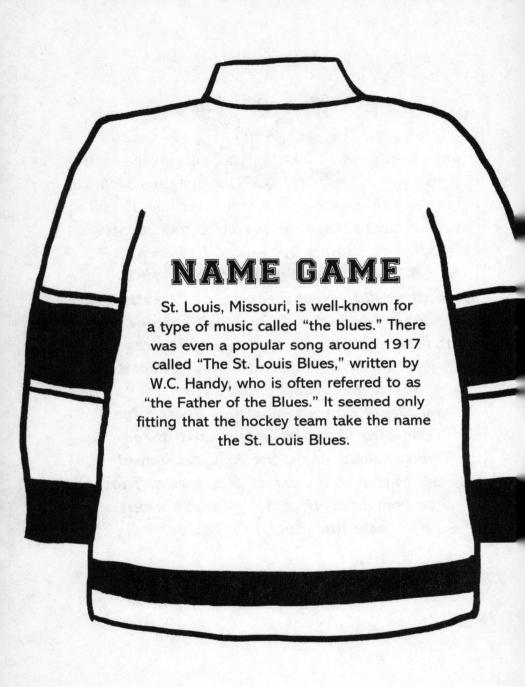

NAME GAME

St. Louis, Missouri, is well-known for a type of music called "the blues." There was even a popular song around 1917 called "The St. Louis Blues," written by W.C. Handy, who is often referred to as "the Father of the Blues." It seemed only fitting that the hockey team take the name the St. Louis Blues.

Working Overtime

The Toronto Maple Leafs and Boston Bruins were the two best teams in the NHL during the 1932–33 season. It was not surprising that their semifinal playoff series that year was a close one. In fact, the first three games of the best-of-five series each went into overtime. The fifth and final game was played on April 3, 1933. It went into overtime too.

Boston and Toronto played three gruelling 20-minute overtime periods that night. That's like playing another full hockey game! Still nobody scored. Finally, in the fourth extra period, Toronto's King Clancy put the puck past Boston goalie Tiny Thompson — but a whistle had sounded just before Clancy shot. No goal.

After a fifth scoreless overtime session, NHL president Frank Calder said the teams should toss a coin to decide the winner. Another suggestion was to continue the game without any goalies. The players on both teams were exhausted, but they decided to play on until somebody won the game fair and square.

Finally, four-and-a-half minutes into the sixth overtime period, Maple Leafs forward Ken Doraty took a pass from Andy Blair. He went wide around the Boston defence and scored! Toronto won the game 1–0 after 104 minutes and 46 seconds of overtime.

Only one game in NHL history has ever lasted longer than the Toronto-Boston playoff game in 1933. In 1936, the Montreal Maroons beat the Detroit Red Wings in a game that lasted 116 minutes and 30 seconds of overtime.

Hockey Knight in Canada?

In 1899, Queen's University challenged the Montreal Shamrocks for the Stanley Cup. Even back then, hockey was a rough game. A newspaper in Quebec City warned that the University boys should order suits of armour and a bunch of coffins for their players, "in order to be prepared for all emergencies."

CUP CAPERS

After losing in 1903 and 1905, the Rat Portage Thistles finally won the Stanley Cup in 1907. By that time, their tiny hometown in northwestern Ontario had been renamed Kenora. With a population of about 6,000 people, it is by far the smallest town ever to boast a Stanley Cup champion.

Kenora beat the Montreal Wanderers to win the Stanley Cup in January 1907. That March, the Wanderers challenged for a rematch. During negotiations to arrange the series, a team official from Kenora got so angry that he threatened to throw the Stanley Cup into the nearby Lake of the Woods! Cooler heads prevailed, and the Cup was saved . . . though the Thistles lost it to the Wanderers, which also gave Kenora the distinction of having the shortest reign as Stanley Cup champions.

No Ordinary Joe

Joe Thornton was the first player in NHL history to lead the league in scoring during a season in which he got traded. Thornton began the 2005–06 season with the Boston Bruins and finished it with the San Jose Sharks. Thornton finished the year with 125 points, edging out the New York Rangers' Jaromir Jagr (who had 123 points) to win the Art Ross Trophy.

ON THE ROAD WITH STANLEY

Mike Richards of the Los Angeles Kings brought the Stanley Cup to his hometown of Kenora, Ontario, in the summer of 2012. While there, he posed for a picture with it beneath a plaque commemorating the 1907 Stanley Cup victory of the Kenora Thistles.

ON THE ROAD WITH STANLEY

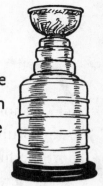

When Scott Niedermayer won the Stanley Cup for the first time with the New Jersey Devils in 1995, he brought the Cup to his hometown in Cranbrook, British Columbia, and hiked with it up to the top of a mountain outside the city. In 2007, when Scott and his brother Rob won the Cup with the Anaheim Ducks, they flew it to the peak of Bull Mountain in a helicopter and posed for pictures on the glacier at the top.

On March 20, 1971, two brothers faced each other in the nets for the only time in NHL history. Ken Dryden's Montreal Canadiens beat Dave Dryden's Buffalo Sabres 5–2.

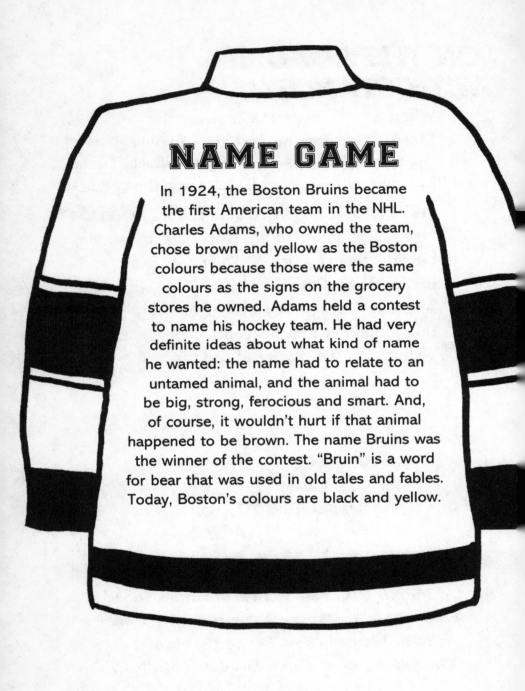

NAME GAME

In 1924, the Boston Bruins became the first American team in the NHL. Charles Adams, who owned the team, chose brown and yellow as the Boston colours because those were the same colours as the signs on the grocery stores he owned. Adams held a contest to name his hockey team. He had very definite ideas about what kind of name he wanted: the name had to relate to an untamed animal, and the animal had to be big, strong, ferocious and smart. And, of course, it wouldn't hurt if that animal happened to be brown. The name Bruins was the winner of the contest. "Bruin" is a word for bear that was used in old tales and fables. Today, Boston's colours are black and yellow.

Dryden Versus Dryden

Ken Dryden of the Montreal Canadiens was one of the best goalies in NHL history. In his eight NHL seasons, he won the Stanley Cup six times. He also won the Vezina Trophy as the league's top goalie five times.

Dave Dryden made his NHL debut on February 3, 1962. He was a junior goalie in Toronto and was watching the game at Maple Leaf Gardens when New York Rangers goalie Gump Worsley got hurt. Teams didn't carry spare goalies back then, so the two teams agreed to let Dave take over.

In the 1970–71 season, Dave was a backup goalie with the Buffalo Sabres; the Canadiens had recently called up Ken from the minors. When the two teams met on March 20, Sabres coach Punch Imlach sent Dave out to start. He thought the Canadiens would start Ken too. When they didn't, Imlach pulled Dave after the first whistle. However, when Canadiens starting goalie Rogie Vachon got injured in the second period, Ken took over. The Sabres put Dave back in the net. When the game was over, and Ken Dryden's Canadiens had won 5–2, fans cheered as the Dryden brothers shook hands at centre ice.

NHL on Board

Professional athletes had been allowed to play hockey at the Winter Olympics since 1988, but the first time that the NHL truly got involved with the Olympics was at the 1998 Winter Games in Nagano, Japan. The NHL shut down its schedule for two weeks in February of 1998 so that its players could join their various national teams.

Olympic Gold and Stanley Silver

In 1980, defenceman Ken Morrow became the first player to win an Olympic gold medal and a Stanley Cup Championship in the same year. Morrow was a member of the American Olympic team that captured a surprising gold medal at Lake Placid that February. After the Olympics, Morrow joined the New York Islanders and won the Stanley Cup in May.

DID YOU KNOW?

When hockey made its first appearance at the Olympics, it was part of a spring sports festival held prior to the start of the 1920 Summer Olympics in Antwerp, Belgium. The Winnipeg Falcons represented Canada that year. They beat Czechoslovakia 15–0, the United States 2–0 and Sweden 12–1 to bring the gold medal home to Canada.

Women of Winter

Women's hockey made its first appearance at the Winter Olympics in Nagano, Japan, in 1998. Before that, four official Women's World Championship tournaments had been held between 1990 and 1997. In every World tournament, Canada had beaten the United States in the final. The two countries met again in the gold medal game at the Olympics, but this time the United States won. In recent years, the Americans have won several World Championships, but the Canadian women have won Olympic gold in 2002, 2006, 2010 and 2014.

One of a Kind

Only one player in hockey history — Connie Broden — has won a gold medal at the World Championship and won the Stanley Cup in the same season. Broden won the 1958 World Championship with the Whitby Dunlops, who represented Canada that year. Just six weeks later, Broden joined the Montreal Canadiens on their march to the Stanley Cup. Although Broden had been a star player with Whitby and was the top scorer at the World Championship tournament with 12 goals and seven assists in seven games, he saw very little action with the Canadiens. In fact, Broden only played in one of the five games against Boston in the Stanley Cup Finals that year. Still, it was enough to get his name engraved on the famous trophy.

Nowadays, a feat like Broden's is impossible. Since 1977, when active NHL players were allowed to compete at the World Championship, the event has always taken place during the Stanley Cup playoffs. That means only players whose NHL teams didn't make the playoffs (or get knocked out early) have a chance to play at the World Championship.

DID YOU KNOW?

During the 2013–14 season, Drew Doughty and Jeff Carter won gold medals for Canada at the Winter Olympics and later won the Stanley Cup with the Los Angeles Kings. As members of the Swedish National Team, Henrik Lundqvist and Carl Hagelin lost the Olympic gold medal game to Canada. They also lost the Stanley Cup Finals to the Kings as members of the New York Rangers. At least they got a silver medal at the Olympics!

Hockey App-titude

Gillian Apps was barely 18 years old when she tried out for the Canadian Women's National Team ahead of the 2002 Winter Olympics. She didn't make the team that year, but she did crack the lineup for the 2004 World Championships. She was one of the top scorers for Canada's Olympic women's hockey team when they won the gold medal in 2006 and has gone on to become one of the longest-serving members of the team. Apps has attracted a lot of attention because she's part of a famous hockey family: her grandfather Syl Apps is a member of the Hockey Hall of Fame. He starred with the Toronto Maple Leafs in the 1930s and '40s and won the Stanley Cup three times. Gillian's father (Syl Apps Jr.) was a star player with the Pittsburgh Penguins in the 1970s.

Stanley Cup Comeback

In the Stanley Cup Finals in 1942, the Toronto Maple Leafs fell behind the Detroit Red Wings three games to nothing. They rallied to win the next four in a row and won the Stanley Cup four games to three.

No other team in NHL history has ever come back to win the Stanley Cup after losing the first three games of the final series.

Born in the U.S.A.

The first American player to be selected first overall in the NHL Entry Draft was Brian Lawton in 1983. The Minnesota North Stars drafted him right out of high school. Lawton is also the first and only high school player ever to be chosen with the number one pick in the draft.

Twin Talents

Not only have there been many brothers who have played together in the NHL, but there have also been six sets of twins!

The first twins to play in the NHL were the two youngest of the six Sutter brothers who played in the league. Rich and Ron Sutter both broke into the NHL in 1982–83. Rich was with the Pittsburgh Penguins and Ron played for the Philadelphia Flyers. They faced each other in a game 17 times in their careers, but were also teammates for two seasons with the St. Louis Blues.

Patrik Sundstrom broke into the NHL with the Vancouver Canucks the same season that the Sutter twins made their NHL debuts. A year later, in 1983–84, Patrik's twin brother Peter joined the New York Rangers. The Sundstrom twins faced each other 18 times in their careers, but were also teammates briefly with the New Jersey Devils in 1989–90.

Twins Chris and Peter Ferraro saw limited action in the NHL between 1995 and 2002. They were teammates for most of their brief careers and never played in a game against each other. Neither have twins Daniel and Henrik Sedin, who have been teammates since they entered the NHL together with the Vancouver Canucks in 2000–01. The Sedins are the only twins, and just the third set of brothers, who have both been the NHL's scoring leader.

On December 14, 2006, Henrik Lundqvist was in net for the New York Rangers against the Dallas Stars. Playing centre for the Stars that night was a rookie who had just been called up from the minors — Henrik's twin, Joel. The Lundqvists became the third set of twins to play against each other in the NHL, but their meeting marked the first time that one twin was a goalie and the other was a forward.

The most recent set of NHL twins is Ryan and Kris Russell. Kris has seen regular duty in the NHL since the 2007–08 season. Ryan has played mostly in the minors, but the two brothers were briefly teammates in the NHL with the Colombus Blue Jackets in 2011–12.

BY THE NUMBERS

Five players have won the
Conn Smythe Trophy as playoff
MVP even though their teams
lost in the Finals:

Year	Name, Position
1966	Roger Crozier, Goalie
1968	Glenn Hall, Goalie
1976	Reggie Leach, Right Wing
1987	Ron Hextall, Goalie
2003	Jean-Sebastien Giguere, Goalie

Team	Winning Team
Detroit Red Wings	Montreal Canadiens
St. Louis Blues	Montreal Canadiens
Philadelphia Flyers	Montreal Canadiens
Philadelphia Flyers	Edmonton Oilers
Anaheim Ducks	New Jersey Devils

Staal in the Family

They don't have six to match the Sutters, but the four Staal brothers of Thunder Bay, Ontario, have all made it to the NHL. As boys, Eric, Marc, Jordan and Jared Staal played hockey together on a backyard rink built by their father.

Eric, the oldest of the Staal brothers, reached the NHL first with the Carolina Hurricanes. The Hurricanes selected him with the second pick in the 2003 NHL Entry Draft, and he made it to the NHL right out of junior hockey in 2003–04. By 2005–06, Eric had become one of the top young stars in the game.

Shortly after Eric won the Stanley Cup with Carolina in 2006, Jordan got drafted into the NHL. Just like Eric, he was picked second overall. Also like Eric, Jordan jumped to the NHL right away. He scored 29 goals as a rookie with the Pittsburgh Penguins in 2006–07 and won the Stanley Cup with the Penguins in 2009. Then Jordan joined Eric on the Hurricanes in 2012.

Marc Staal is a year older than Jordan, but it took him a little longer to reach the NHL. The New York Rangers had selected him with the 12th pick in the 2005 NHL Entry Draft, but he didn't reach the NHL until the 2007–08 season. The only Staal brother who isn't a forward, Marc is a solid defenceman.

Jared is the youngest of the Staal brothers. He was selected by the Coyotes in the second round of the 2008 NHL Entry Draft but was later traded to Carolina. He hasn't played much in the NHL, but his debut was one to remember! Jared played his first game with the Hurricanes on April 25, 2013. He wore number 13 and played right wing on a line with Eric (number 12) and Jordan (number 11). The opponents that night were the New York Rangers. Unfortunately, Marc was injured at the time or else all four Staal brothers could have seen action in the same game.

Malkin's Magic

When Evgeni Malkin joined the Pittsburgh Penguins in 2006–07, he set a modern rookie record by scoring a goal in each of his first six NHL games. Nobody else had begun his NHL career with such a scoring streak since the league's very first season of 1917–18!

Red Rover

In the early days of hockey, teams had seven players on the ice instead of six. In addition to a goalie, two defencemen and three forwards, teams had a rover between the forwards and the defencemen. The National Hockey Association was the first league in hockey to get rid of the rover, which they did before the 1911–12 season. Problem was, when the Pacific Coast Hockey Association started up that season, they decided to keep the rover. So when the two leagues began competing for the Stanley Cup, the rules would switch back and forth for every game. The leagues also had different rules about passing and offside, so it was a lot for everyone to keep track of!

CUP CHRONICLES

In 1915, the Vancouver Millionaires became the first PCHA team to win the Stanley Cup. Their victory marked the first time the Stanley Cup had travelled west of Winnipeg. British Columbia celebrated a second championship in 1925 when the Victoria Cougars won the Cup. They would be the last champions from the West Coast until the Anaheim Ducks won the Stanley Cup in 2007.

ON THE ROAD WITH STANLEY

After winning the Stanley Cup with the Carolina Hurricanes in 2006, Eric Staal brought it home to Thunder Bay. But none of his three younger brothers would go near it. They didn't want to jinx their own chances of winning it some day.

When Jordan Staal won the Cup with Pittsburgh in 2009, he slept with it at night, ate a bowlful of Frosted Flakes out of it in the morning and later enjoyed an ice cream sundae out of it. Makes you wonder what brothers Marc and Jared Staal have planned if they ever win it!

BY THE NUMBERS

The record for the most goals by one team in a single NHL game is held by the Montreal Canadiens. On March 3, 1920, the Canadiens beat the Quebec Bulldogs 16–3. Here is a look at the highest-scoring games in NHL history:

Goals	Teams/Score
21	Montreal Canadiens 14, Toronto St. Patricks 7
	Edmonton Oilers 12, Chicago Blackhawks 9
20	Edmonton Oilers 12, Minnesota North Stars 8
	Toronto Maple Leafs 11, Edmonton Oilers 9
19	Montreal Wanderers 10, Toronto Arenas 9
	Montreal Canadiens 16, Quebec Bulldogs 3
	Montreal Canadiens 13, Hamilton Tigers 6
	Boston Bruins 10, New York Rangers 9
	Detroit Red Wings 10, Boston Bruins 9
	Vancouver Canucks 10, Minnesota North Stars 9

Date

January 10, 1920

December 11, 1985

January 4, 1984

January 8, 1986

December 19, 1917

March 3, 1920

February 26, 1921

March 4, 1944

March 16, 1944

October 7, 1983

DID YOU KNOW?

The NHL record for the most points by one player in a single game is 10! Darryl Sittler had six goals and four assists for the Toronto Maple Leafs on February 7, 1976. The Leafs beat the Boston Bruins 11–4 that night.

Darryl Sittler of the Toronto Maple Leafs

Son of Stastny

Paul Stastny was a rookie sensation with the Colorado Avalanche in 2006–07. In fact, he set an NHL rookie record by scoring a point in 20 straight games from February 3 to March 17, 2007. Overall, Stastny had 28 goals and 50 assists in his rookie season. His 78 points gave him the fourth-highest rookie total in Colorado franchise history. Who were the only franchise rookies to score more points than Paul Stastny? His father Peter Stastny and his uncles Anton and Marion, back when the Avalanche were still the Quebec Nordiques!

Sidney Sittler?

Sidney Crosby has kind of an odd nickname — Darryl, as in Darryl Sittler. He earned it during his very first exhibition game with the Rimouski Oceanic in the Quebec Major Junior Hockey League. Crosby had four goals and four assists in that game. People started calling him Darryl after that because of Sittler's NHL scoring record.

Just Win, Baby!

In 1986, Chris Nilan of the Montreal Canadiens took a picture of his baby son sitting inside the Stanley Cup bowl. "His bottom fit right in," said the noted hockey tough guy. In 1996, Colorado Avalanche defenceman Sylvain Lefebvre christened his new baby in the bowl of the Cup. After Detroit won in 2008, Kris Draper put his newborn baby daughter in the bowl, and things got a little messy! "She pooped in the Cup," Draper explained. "But I still drank out of it that night, so no worries." Kris's older kids later ate Timbits out of the Stanley Cup, so it must have been pretty clean by then.

After wheeling and dealing with the Islanders, Tampa and Atlanta, Vancouver wound up with the second and third picks in the 1999 NHL Entry Draft. They used the two picks to select twin brothers Daniel and Henrik Sedin. The Sedins have gone on to become the two top point scorers in Canucks history.

Pucks Versus Pitching

When Wayne Gretzky was a boy, he liked baseball even more than hockey. He pitched and played shortstop on local baseball teams while growing up in Brantford, Ontario. Gretzky was already such a great hockey player that newspaper reporters were interviewing him when he was only 10 years old. In his very first interview in 1971, Gretzky said he would like to be playing baseball with the Oakland A's and their star pitcher Vida Blue.

The most goals ever scored against a team in an NHL shutout game is 15. The Detroit Red Wings beat the New York Rangers 15–0 on January 23, 1944.

Road Woes

Two teams in modern NHL history have gone an entire season with only one win on the road. Both were expansion teams in their very first season. The 1974–75 Washington Capitals were 1–39–0 on the road. The 1992–93 Ottawa Senators were 1–41–0.

BY THE NUMBERS

Longest Consecutive Goal-Scoring Streak

Games	Player, Team
16	Punch Broadbent, Ottawa Senators
14	Joe Malone, Montreal Canadiens
13	Newsy Lalonde, Montreal Canadiens
	Charlie Simmer, Los Angeles Kings
12	Cy Denneny, Ottawa Senators
	Dave Lumley, Edmonton Oilers
	Mario Lemieux, Pittsburgh Penguins

Longest Consecutive Assist Streak

Games	Player, Team
23	Wayne Gretzky, Los Angeles Kings
18	Adam Oates, Boston Bruins
17	Wayne Gretzky, Edmonton Oilers
	Paul Coffey, Edmonton Oilers
	Wayne Gretzky, Los Angeles Kings
16	Jaromir Jagr, Pittsburgh Penguins

Season

1921–22

1917–18

1920–21

1979–80

1917–18

1981–82

1992–93

Season

1990–91

1992–93

1983–84

1985–86

1989–90

2000–01

BY THE NUMBERS

Longest Consecutive Point Streak

Games	Player, Team
51	Wayne Gretzky, Edmonton Oilers
46	Mario Lemieux, Pittsburgh Penguins
39	Wayne Gretzky, Edmonton Oilers
30	Wayne Gretzky, Edmonton Oilers
	Mats Sundin, Quebec Nordiques

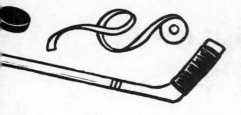

Season
1983–84
1989–90
1985–86
1982–83
1992–93

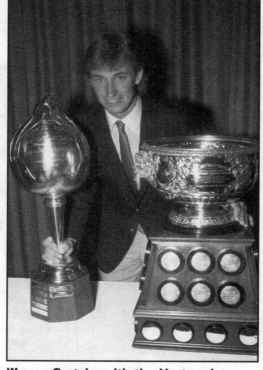

Wayne Gretzky with the Hart and Art Ross Trophies

Making History . . . Twice

On October 11, 2007, Mats Sundin became the top-scoring player in the history of the Toronto Maple Leafs. In fact, he broke the team scoring record twice in the same game! Well, sort of . . .

Sundin entered the game that night tied with Darryl Sittler for the all-time Leafs lead with 389 goals and 916 points. During the second period, Sundin was given credit for an assist on a Toronto goal. That gave him 917 points. The game was held up for several minutes while the fans at the Air Canada Centre cheered.

Sundin saluting the crowd at the end of the game

There was just one problem. Sundin knew that he hadn't actually touched the puck on the play. He didn't deserve the assist. Early in the third period, it was announced that the assist had been taken away. Sundin no longer had the record. But a few minutes later, he had it again. In fact, Sundin scored a goal this time, giving him 390 goals and 917 points to set new Leafs records in both categories.

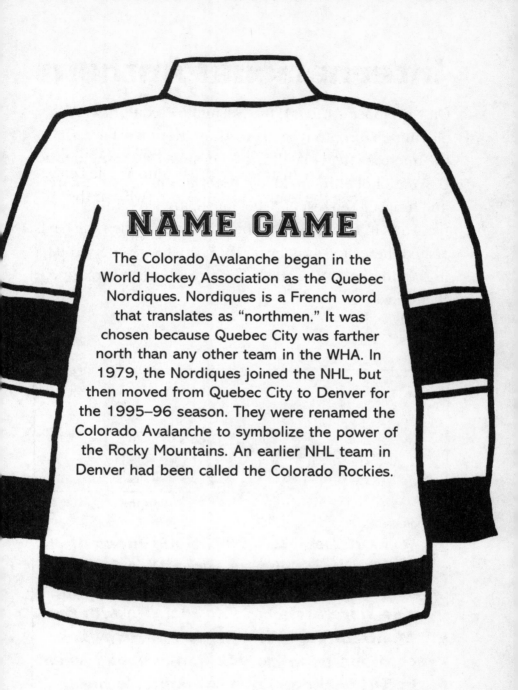

NAME GAME

The Colorado Avalanche began in the World Hockey Association as the Quebec Nordiques. Nordiques is a French word that translates as "northmen." It was chosen because Quebec City was farther north than any other team in the WHA. In 1979, the Nordiques joined the NHL, but then moved from Quebec City to Denver for the 1995–96 season. They were renamed the Colorado Avalanche to symbolize the power of the Rocky Mountains. An earlier NHL team in Denver had been called the Colorado Rockies.

International Anthem

On November 18, 2014, the Nashville Predators were playing in Toronto when something went wrong with the microphone while the anthem singer was singing the U.S. national anthem. Maple Leafs fans jumped right in and finished the rest of "The Star-Spangled Banner" for her. Fans in Nashville returned the favour when the Leafs visited there on February 3, 2015. Predators fans joined in the singing of "O Canada" and even sang a verse by themselves.

On October 10, 1987, Doug Jarvis of the Hartford Whalers played his 964th consecutive game, having never missed a game since breaking into the NHL with the Montreal Canadiens in 1975. His NHL-record "ironman" streak finally ended when he sat out the very next night. He never played another game in the NHL after that.

BY THE NUMBERS

In 1926, the Montreal Maroons won the Stanley Cup after just two seasons in the NHL. Two years later, the New York Rangers won the Stanley Cup in their second season. The NHL would not add any more expansion teams until the 1967–68 season. Since then, only three teams have won the Stanley Cup in under 10 years. Those teams are:

Team	First Season	First Cup
Edmonton Oilers	1979–80	1983–84
Philadelphia Flyers	1967–68	1973–74
New York Islanders	1972–73	1979–80

Starry, Starry (Starry) Night

On the night he broke the Maple Leafs' scoring record, Mats Sundin was selected as the first, second and third star of the game. Many years before, on March 23, 1944, Montreal Canadiens legend Maurice "Rocket" Richard had been named all three stars in a game against Toronto. Richard scored all five Montreal goals that night as the Canadiens beat the Maple Leafs 5–1.

John Grahame is the only player in hockey history to have had his name on the Stanley Cup along with his mother. Grahame was a backup goalie for Tampa Bay when they won the Stanley Cup in 2004. His mother, Charlotte Grahame, worked in the front office for Colorado when they won the Cup in 2001.

Gold Was Great

For Canadians, it was an amazing victory. For Americans, it was a heartbreaking loss. When it was over, the gold medal game at the 2014 Winter Olympics may have been the greatest comeback in the history of women's hockey!

For 56 minutes and 34 seconds, Team U.S.A. seemed to have the win well in hand. They were leading Team Canada 2–0 and their goalie, Jessie Vetter, looked unbeatable. Then, with 3:26 remaining, Brianne Jenner finally got Canada on the scoreboard. The Canadians pulled their goalie, and the Americans just missed clinching the game when a long, slow shot bounced off Canada's goalpost. Canada was still alive. With just 55 seconds to go, Canada's Marie-Philip Poulin snapped in a shot for the tying goal. It would take overtime to decide the winner. American star Hilary Knight was in the penalty box when Poulin scored her second goal of the game at 8:10 of the extra period, giving Team Canada a thrilling 3–2 victory — and their fourth straight Olympic gold.

BY THE NUMBERS

The 1976–77 Montreal Canadiens still hold the NHL record of 132 points in a season, even though their mark of 60 wins is no longer the best. Here's a look at the NHL teams with the most wins and the ones with the most losses in one season:

Most Wins	Team, Season
62	Detroit Red Wings, 1995–96
60	Montreal Canadiens, 1976–77
59	Montreal Canadiens, 1977–78

Most Losses	Team, Season
71	San Jose Sharks, 1992–93
70	Ottawa Senators, 1992–93
67	Washington Capitals, 1974–75

Wins, Losses, Ties
(62–13–7, 131 points)
(60–8–12, 132 points)
(59–10–11, 129 points)

Wins, Losses, Ties
(11–71–2, 24 points)
(10–70–4, 24 points)
(8–67–5, 21 points)

NHL Overseas

The first regular-season NHL games to be played outside
of North America were played in Japan. The Vancouver
Canucks and the Anaheim Ducks opened the 1997–98
NHL season with a pair of games at Tokyo's Yoyogi
Arena. One year later, the San Jose Sharks and the
Calgary Flames opened the 1998–99 season with two
more games in the Japanese capital.

Ten years after their trip to Japan, the Ducks took
part in the first NHL regular-season games to be played
in Europe. The Ducks and the Los Angeles Kings opened
the 2007–08 season with two games at the O2 Arena in
London, England.

Oh, Brother!

Four sets of brothers once appeared on the ice in a
single NHL game! It was a game between the New York
Rangers and Chicago Black Hawks on December 1,
1940. Lynn and Muzz Patrick and Neil and Mac Colville
were teammates together on the Rangers. Max and
Doug Bentley and Bob and Bill Carse all played for the
Black Hawks.

Gentleman of Japan

On January 13, 2007, Yutaka Fukufuji became the first person born in Japan to play a game in the NHL. Fukufuji was a goalie with the Los Angeles Kings. He played the third period of a game that night against the Vancouver Canucks. Three nights later, Fukufuji got his first start against the Atlanta Thrashers. In all, he played four games for the Kings in 2006–07, but spent most of the season in the minor leagues.

Fukufuji was born in Tokyo on September 17, 1982, and played for the Kokudo Tokyo team in the Asian ice hockey league. He moved to North America in 2004 after being drafted by the Kings.

On January 22, 1987, a snowstorm in New Jersey delayed the start of the game between the Devils and Flames for 106 minutes. Only 334 fans fought their way through the 38 cm (15 in.) of snow to see the game, which the Devils won 7–5.

Thanks, but No Thanks

In 1950, the Detroit Red Wings won the Stanley Cup with Harry Lumley as their goalie. Lumley would eventually make it to the Hockey Hall of Fame, but the Red Wings thought they could do better. After the season, they traded Lumley to Chicago and called up Terry Sawchuk from the minors. Sawchuk became one of the greatest goalies in NHL history. He helped Detroit win the Stanley Cup in 1952, 1954 and 1955 . . . but then Detroit traded him away too. It would take 42 years before the Red Wings won the Stanley Cup again in 1997. Mike Vernon was their goalie that year, but guess what? The Red Wings traded him that summer!

DID YOU KNOW?

The longest game ever played in the Stanley Cup Finals took place on May 15 and 16, 1990. Petr Klima scored at 15:13 of triple overtime to give the Edmonton Oilers a 3–2 win over Boston.

Clancy Kept It

When the Ottawa Senators won the Stanley Cup
in 1923, defenceman King Clancy asked the team
executives if he could bring it home. Clancy wanted
to show the Stanley Cup to his father, who had been
a star athlete himself. The next season, NHL president
Frank Calder asked the Senators to return the Cup.
The problem was, none of the team executives could
find it! After a while, Clancy admitted the Stanley Cup
was still at his house, sitting on his mantel.

One, Two, Three

The 2006–07 season was the first time in NHL history that the players who finished first, second and third in the scoring race had all once been first-round NHL draft picks. Sidney Crosby — who won the Art Ross Trophy that year — was the first pick in 2005, Joe Thornton was first in 1997 and Vincent Lecavalier was first in 1998.

Punch's Pretend Pick

In the 1974 NHL Entry Draft, Buffalo Sabres general manager Punch Imlach selected an imaginary Japanese player. Taro Tsujimoto was supposedly a centre with the Tokyo Katanas of the Japanese Hockey League. The Sabres selected him in the 11th round, 183rd overall. A few weeks later, the NHL discovered that Tsujimoto didn't really exist. Imlach later admitted that he had played the prank because of his frustration over how long the draft was dragging on. Today NHL records list the 183rd selection of the 1974 Draft as an "invalid claim."

How Swede It Is

The first European-trained player to be chosen number-one overall in the NHL Entry Draft was Mats Sundin of Sweden. Sundin was picked first by the Quebec Nordiques in 1989.

Firsts From Russia

Ilya Kovalchuk became the first Russian to be selected first overall in the NHL Entry Draft when the Atlanta Thrashers picked him in 2001. Alex Ovechkin was the second player from Russia to go first overall when the Washington Capitals selected him with the top pick in 2004.

The Very First

The first player selected in the very first NHL Draft back in 1963 was Garry Monahan. The 16-year-old was picked by the Montreal Canadiens. It took him four years before he finally made his NHL debut. Monahan wound up only playing 14 games for Montreal, although he did go on to enjoy a 12-year career in the NHL.

Only three goalies have ever been selected first overall in the NHL Entry Draft: Michel Plasse (Montreal Canadiens, 1968), Rick DiPietro (New York Islanders, 2000) and Marc-Andre Fleury (Pittsburgh, 2003).

It Was a Long One . . .

The 2000 NHL Entry Draft featured the most players ever picked in draft history. In all, 293 players were selected that year. The very last player picked in the longest draft ever was Lauri Kinos of Finland. Kinos never made it to the NHL.

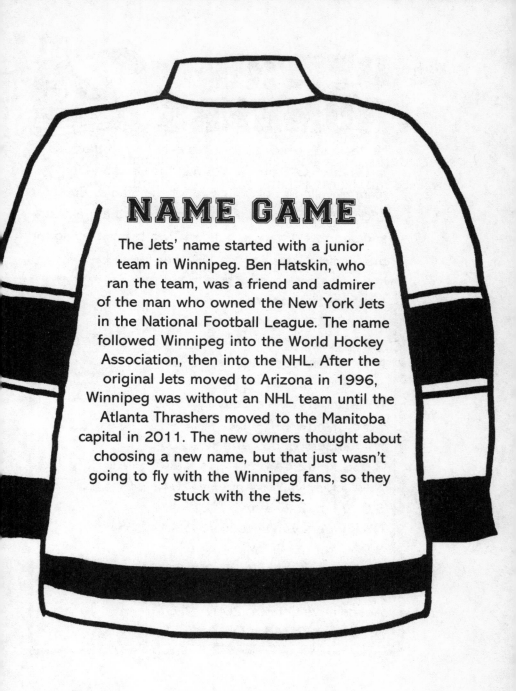

NAME GAME

The Jets' name started with a junior team in Winnipeg. Ben Hatskin, who ran the team, was a friend and admirer of the man who owned the New York Jets in the National Football League. The name followed Winnipeg into the World Hockey Association, then into the NHL. After the original Jets moved to Arizona in 1996, Winnipeg was without an NHL team until the Atlanta Thrashers moved to the Manitoba capital in 2011. The new owners thought about choosing a new name, but that just wasn't going to fly with the Winnipeg fans, so they stuck with the Jets.

BY THE NUMBERS

No team in hockey history has ever had to travel as far as the 6,000 km (3,728 mi.) the Dawson City team travelled to play Ottawa for the Stanley Cup back in 1905. Here's a look at some of the greatest and shortest distances between two teams playing for the Stanley Cup since the NHL was formed:

Greatest Distances

Boston vs Vancouver, 2011
4,027 km (2,502 mi.)
Montreal vs Los Angeles, 1993
3,973 km (2,469 mi.)
NY Islanders vs Vancouver, 1982
3,937 km (2,446 mi.)
NY Rangers vs Los Angeles, 2014
3,933 km (2,444 mi.)
New Jersey vs Los Angeles, 2012
3,919 km (2,435 mi.)
NY Rangers vs Vancouver, 1994
3,906 km (2,427 mi.)
New Jersey vs Anaheim, 2003
3,906 km (2,427 mi.)
Anaheim vs Ottawa, 2007
3,771 km (2,343 mi.)

Montreal vs Victoria, 1925, 1926
3,731 km (2,318 mi.)
Tampa Bay vs Calgary, 2004
3,687 km (2,291 mi.)
Seattle vs Montreal, 1919
3,687 km (2,291 mi.)
Toronto vs Vancouver, 1918
3,362 km (2,089 mi.)

Shortest Distances
Philadelphia vs NY Islanders, 1980
162 km (100 mi.)
Boston vs NY Rangers, 1929, 1972
303 km (189 mi.)
Detroit vs Pittsburgh, 2008, 2009
331 km (206 mi.)
Toronto vs Detroit, numerous times
333 km (207 mi.)
Detroit vs Chicago, 1934, 1961
385 km (239 mi.)

(all distances are estimates)

Jinx!

Hockey players seem to have an awful lot of superstitions. But the Stanley Cup has its own special set of traditions and superstitions. One of the most obvious to fans is the tradition of the playoff beard. Many players refuse to shave during the playoffs. This tradition is thought to have started with the New York Islanders in the 1980s. By the time the Finals roll around, there are an awful lot of shaggy faces on the ice!

Many hockey players today believe it's bad luck to touch the Stanley Cup if they haven't won it yet. A growing number of players also believe it's unlucky to pick up the Prince of Wales Trophy or the Clarence Campbell Bowl, the trophies awarded for winning the Eastern and Western conferences.

Superstitious as he was, Wayne Gretzky was always happy to pick up the Clarence Campbell Bowl when the Edmonton Oilers won the Western Conference. "It makes me sad," said The Great One, "that players won't pick up the trophy today. I think it's wrong. They should be happy they won it."

But the conference trophy superstition hasn't always worked out over the years. In 2008, Sidney Crosby refused to touch the Prince of Wales Trophy when the Penguins won the Eastern Conference, and they lost the Stanley Cup to Detroit. A year later, Crosby lifted it . . . and the Penguins ended up winning the Cup when the two teams faced each other for the second year in a row. Meanwhile, Detroit captain Nicklas Lidstrom refused to touch the Campbell Bowl both years, so who knows? And then in 2010, Chicago's Jonathan Toews skated away from the Campbell Bowl while Philadelphia's Mike Richards carried the Wales Trophy to the Flyers' dressing room. Who won the Cup? Chicago.

On March 23, 1994, Wayne Gretzky scored his 802nd NHL career goal to move past Gordie Howe into first place. Commissioner Gary Bettman presented Gretzky with a book containing the score sheets from every game in which he had scored.

The Memorial Cup is the championship trophy for junior hockey in Canada. The Ontario Hockey Association donated the Memorial Cup in 1919 in memory of the many Canadian hockey players who had been killed fighting in World War I.

CUP CHRONICLES

Doug McKay played just one game in his NHL career, but it was a pretty important one: it was during the 1950 Stanley Cup Finals for the Detroit Red Wings. McKay is the only player in history to play his only NHL game with a Cup-winning team during the Stanley Cup Finals.

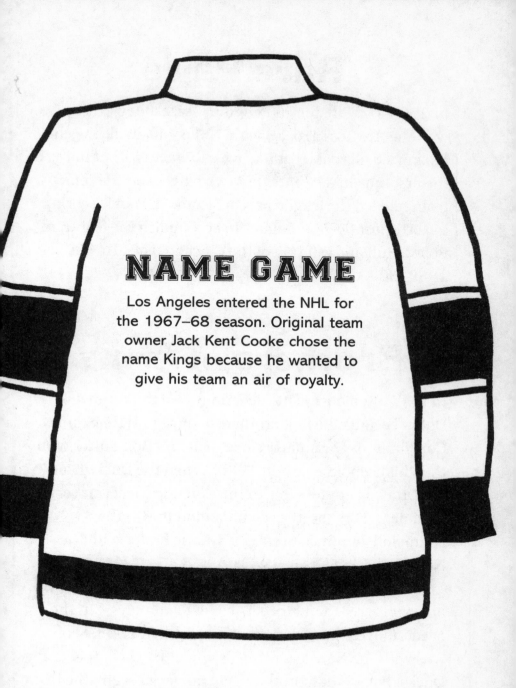

NAME GAME

Los Angeles entered the NHL for the 1967–68 season. Original team owner Jack Kent Cooke chose the name Kings because he wanted to give his team an air of royalty.

Rare Pairs

In 2006–07, Pittsburgh Penguins star Sidney Crosby won the Art Ross Trophy with 120 points while Evgeni Malkin led all rookie scorers with 85 points. That marked the first time in 47 years that two players on the same team had led the league in scoring and in rookie scoring too. The last two teammates to accomplish the feat were Bobby Hull and Bill Hay of the Chicago Black Hawks in 1959–60.

Brothers in Arms

In 2007, Rob and Scott Niedermayer of the Anaheim Ducks became the first brothers to appear in the Stanley Cup Finals as teammates since Rich and Ron Sutter with the Philadelphia Flyers in 1985. When the Ducks beat the Ottawa Senators to win the Cup, the Niedermayers became the first brother combination to win the championship since Brent and Duane Sutter with the New York Islanders in 1983.

Brothers facing each other in the Stanley Cup Finals are even rarer than brothers being teammates, but the Niedermayers have done that too! Back in 2003, Scott was with the New Jersey Devils when they beat the Ducks. Before that, brothers had not faced each other in the battle for the Stanley Cup since Ken Reardon's Montreal Canadiens beat Terry Reardon's Boston Bruins way back in 1946.

Brothers Versus Brothers

In the second round of the 2007 playoffs, Rob and Scott Niedermayer of the Anaheim Ducks played against Henrik and Daniel Sedin of the Vancouver Canucks. It was the first time since 1986 that each team in a playoff series featured a pair of brothers. Back then, Peter and Anton Stastny of the Quebec Nordiques played Dave and Wayne Babych of the Hartford Whalers.

Four of a Kind

Only one family in history has produced four hockey-playing brothers that all got their names on the Stanley Cup: the Bouchers. George, Frank, Billy and Bobby all had their names engraved on the treasured mug (some more than once) between 1927 and 1940.

Pay Up!

When the Wanderers won the championship in 1910, they never actually received it. In those days, the winning team had to put up a bond for $1,000 to guarantee they would not damage the Cup. The Wanderers had a new owner in 1910, and he didn't know about that rule. He never put up the bond, so the Wanderers never received the trophy!

Flat Tire

One of the most famous stories about the Stanley Cup's early adventures is from 1924. The Montreal Canadiens won the Cup that year, and team owner Leo Dandurand invited the players over to his house for a private victory party. A carload of players was taking the Cup to Dandurand's place when they got a flat tire. The players got out to make the repairs and put the Cup on the curb beside them. When they finally arrived at Dandurand's house, they realized they had left the Stanley Cup behind! So they got back in the car, and once again drove through the streets of Montreal. Lucky for them, they found the Cup right where they left it, still sitting on the curb.

Odie Cleghorn, a star player in hockey's early days, is credited as being the first coach to change his lines "on the fly." Cleghorn coached the NHL's Pittsburgh Pirates from 1925 to 1929. Before Cleghorn's innovation, most coaches liked to play their top stars for as much of the game as possible. Even the coaches who did make line changes back then always made them after a whistle had stopped the play.

Big, Bad Bruins

Bobby Orr was just 18 years old when he joined the
Boston Bruins in 1966. The following year, Phil Esposito
was traded to the team. At that time, the Bruins had
missed the playoffs for eight straight seasons and hadn't
won the Stanley Cup since 1941. However, with Orr and
"Espo" together, the Bruins were soon the best team in
the league. Together, they won the Stanley Cup in 1970
and 1972.

In 1968–69, Phil Esposito became the first player
in NHL history to reach 100 points in a single season.
He won the Art Ross Trophy that year with 126 points.
But, as good as Esposito was, there are many people
who think that his teammate was the greatest player
ever. Not only was Orr a brilliant defenceman, he was
also one of hockey's best scorers. In fact, he is the only
defenceman in NHL history to win the Art Ross Trophy.
He led the league in scoring twice, first in 1969–70, and
then again in 1974–75. Orr also scored the winning goal
for Boston when they won the Cup in 1970. He won
the Conn Smythe Trophy as the most valuable player
in the playoffs that year, and also won it in 1972 when
Boston won the Stanley Cup again.

The Broad Street Bullies

The Philadelphia Flyers were the roughest team in hockey during the 1970s. Because their home arena was on Broad Street in Philadelphia, local sportswriters dubbed the team "The Broad Street Bullies." Flyers fans would say their team was aggressive, but most other teams just thought they were dirty! Still, the Flyers were talented as well as tough. They won the Stanley Cup in 1974 and again in 1975. When the Anaheim Ducks won the Stanley Cup in 2007, they became the first team since the Flyers in 1975 to lead the league in penalty minutes and win the Stanley Cup in the same season.

BY THE NUMBERS

The record for goals in an NHL season has more than doubled since Joe Malone first set the standard with 44 in the league's first season. Here's how the record has grown over the years:

Goals	Player	Season
44	Joe Malone	1917–18
50	Maurice Richard	1944–45
50	Bernie Geoffrion	1960–61
50	Bobby Hull	1961–62
54	Bobby Hull	1965–66
58	Bobby Hull	1968–69
76	Phil Esposito	1970–71
92	Wayne Gretzky	1981–82

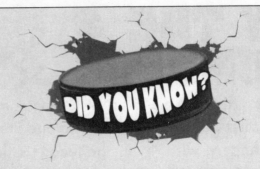

The Wonderful World of Disney

A few days after the Tampa Bay Lightning won the Stanley Cup in 2004, captain Dave Andreychuk and his family took it to nearby Disney World. Mickey Mouse, Minnie Mouse, Pluto and Goofy (dressed in a hockey uniform) all joined the Andreychuks and the Stanley Cup for a parade down Main Street, U.S.A.

Batman

Game 3 of the 1975 Stanley Cup Finals between the Buffalo Sabres and Philadelphia Flyers was a strange one. The temperature was unusually hot for Buffalo that May 20, and the heat caused a thick fog to hover over the ice. Sometimes it was so thick, the game had to be stopped. The players skated circles around the ice, trying to clear the fog, but it didn't really work. It was hard for the goalies to see the puck.

Shortly before the fog rolled in, a bat had been spotted swooping around the ice. The Sabres' Jim Lorentz smacked it out of the air with his stick and killed it. Maybe the fog was the bat's revenge! Sabres fans certainly considered it a bad omen. Buffalo won the game that night, but they went on to lose the series in six games.

BY THE NUMBERS

Wayne Gretzky won the Art Ross Trophy as scoring champion more times than any other player in NHL history. Here is a list of players who have won the Art Ross Trophy the most times:

Player	Wins
Wayne Gretzky	10
Mario Lemieux	6
Gordie Howe	6
Jaromir Jagr	5
Phil Esposito	5
Stan Mikita	4

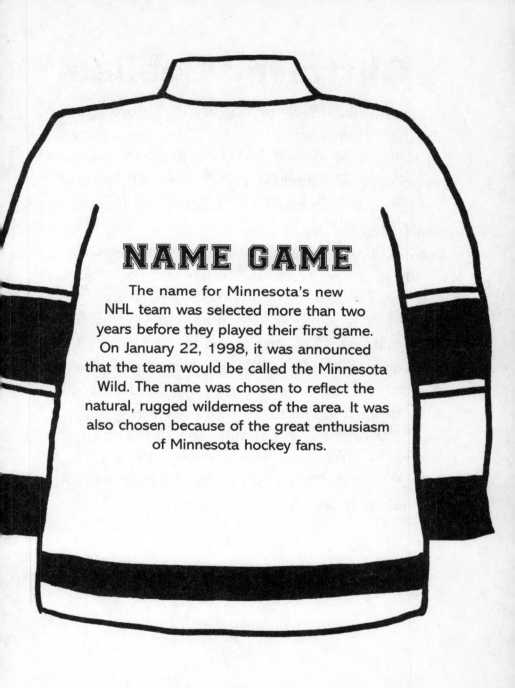

NAME GAME

The name for Minnesota's new NHL team was selected more than two years before they played their first game. On January 22, 1998, it was announced that the team would be called the Minnesota Wild. The name was chosen to reflect the natural, rugged wilderness of the area. It was also chosen because of the great enthusiasm of Minnesota hockey fans.

Glittering Goalies

Patrick Roy was the first goalie in NHL history to win 500 games in his career, doing it with a 2–0 win over the Dallas Stars on December 26, 2001. At the end of his career, Roy had tallied 551 wins; he had 289 with the Montreal Canadiens and 262 with the Colorado Avalanche, making him the only goalie in NHL history to win 200 or more games with two different teams.

On November 17, 2006, Roy got some company in the 500-win club: Martin Brodeur. While he was growing up in Montreal, Brodeur idolized Patrick Roy. Though Brodeur lost three games in a row before finally winning his 500th, he still got to the milestone faster than Roy had. Roy got his 500th win in his 933rd game, while Brodeur got his in his 900th game. Brodeur just kept on winning after that, notching his 600th victory on April 6, 2010. In all, Brodeur won 688 games in 21 seasons with the New Jersey Devils and three more with St. Louis in 2014–15, for a final total of 691 wins.

Luongo Time Coming

Roberto Luongo's teams had never made the playoffs during his first six seasons in the NHL. When he finally did make it with the Vancouver Canucks in 2006–07, it seemed like he was going to make up for all that lost time in a single night!

In his very first playoff game on April 11, 2007, Luongo faced more rubber than any goalie ever had before in his playoff debut. The Dallas Stars fired 76 shots at Luongo that night in a game that went into four overtime periods. Luongo made 72 saves as Vancouver won 5–4. Luongo was just one save short of the record for saves in a single playoff game, which was set by Kelly Hrudey when he played for the New York Islanders. On April 18, 1987, Hrudey made 73 saves as the Islanders beat the Washington Capitals 3–2 in another quadruple overtime game.

Long Time for Trophies

Paul Coffey won the Norris Trophy as the NHL's best defenceman two years in a row, in 1984–85 and 1985–86. He later won the Norris for a third time, but not until nine seasons later, in 1994–95. No one in NHL history had ever won a trophy again after such a lengthy time in between.

Joe Sakic also waited a long time for a trophy win. Though he'd been a top player throughout his career, the Colorado Avalanche star was in his 13th season when he was awarded the Hart Trophy as NHL MVP in 2000–01. No Hart winner in NHL history had played so long in the league before winning the trophy for the first time.

Overtime Overdue

For nearly 50 years, Maurice Richard held the career record for overtime goals in the playoffs. "The Rocket" won six games for the Montreal Canadiens in sudden death situations from 1946 to 1958. Even though teams today can play twice as many playoff games in a year as they did in Richard's time, it took until 2006 for his record to finally be beaten. Colorado Avalanche star Joe Sakic did it with his seventh career overtime goal on April 24, 2006. Sakic scored overtime goal number eight on April 9, 2008.

Hard to Ruffle His Feathers!

Before Roberto Luongo played his first post-season game, Anaheim Ducks goalie Jean-Sebastien Giguere had faced the most shots ever in a playoff debut. Giguere stopped 63 of 64 shots to lead the Ducks past the Detroit Red Wings 2–1 in overtime on April 10, 2003.

Giguere's win for the Ducks that night began one of the most remarkable streaks in playoff history. He won six more games in overtime without a loss during the 2003 playoffs, then won two more overtime games during his next playoff appearance in 2006. By the time he was finally beaten in an overtime game in the first round of the 2007 playoffs, Giguere had set an NHL record by playing 197 minutes and 52 seconds of overtime hockey without allowing a goal. That's like going nearly 10 periods — or more than three full games — without allowing a goal, in hockey's most pressure-packed situation! Giguere certainly didn't let the end of his streak fluster him either. He bounced back to win four more overtime games during the rest of the 2007 playoffs to help lead the Ducks to their first Stanley Cup Championship.

In Case of Emergency

Ever since the 1965–66 season, the NHL has had a rule saying that every team has to have two goalies in uniform for every game on the schedule. But what happens if one of those two goalies gets hurt at the last minute and a minor league replacement can't make it to the arena in time? Teams generally have a list of local goalies they can call in an emergency. In recent history, no emergency goalie has actually made it into an NHL game, but a few sure have come close!

During the first minute of the first period of a game early in the 2013–14 season, James Reimer of the Toronto Maple Leafs got hit in the head and had to come out. Jonathan Bernier took over, but with Reimer injured, who would be Bernier's backup? The Leafs turned to Brett Willows, a goalie with the University of Toronto. Willows was just about to start dinner when he got a call to hurry down to the Air Canada Centre. When he got there, he suited up and was given a Leafs jersey with his name and number 82 on the back. But that was as close as he got to playing in the NHL. Willows wound up watching the rest of the game from the dressing room.

Late in the 2012–13 season, Dustin Butler of the University of Calgary got a call to be the emergency backup goalie for the Vancouver Canucks, who were visiting the Flames. Butler got to sit on the bench, and with Vancouver up 4–1 late in the game, his new teammates were pushing for him to see some action.

Sadly, there was no whistle in the final minute, so Butler never got a chance to get into the game.

Tom Fenton was at a barbershop back in 2010 when he got a call to rush down to Madison Square Garden. Fenton, a coach at Manhattanville College, hadn't played in a game in two years and thought a couple of his buddies were pranking him. This was no joke. The Coyotes were playing the Rangers and couldn't get a minor-league goalie to New York quickly enough, so Fenton had to don his goalie gear as their backup. He almost got into the game when the Coyotes' starting goalie Jason LaBarbera suffered a minor injury. In the end, LaBarbera recovered during a short break in the play, and Fenton was pretty relieved to stay on the bench.

Man's Best Friend

Clark Gillies celebrated the New York Islanders' 1980 Stanley Cup victory by having his picture taken with the prized trophy and his German shepherd, Hombre. There was still a bit of champagne left in the bowl and Hombre quickly slurped it up. Later, Gillies was asked to explain how he could let such a thing happen. "So what?" he said. "He's a good dog."

Jean-Sebastien Giguere did things a little bit differently with his dog when Anaheim won the Stanley Cup in 2007. After letting his golden retriever Henri eat dog food from the bowl of the Cup, Giguere laughed and asked his family and friends, "Anybody want champagne now?"

Rangers Treat It Rough

The New York Rangers celebrated hard after ending their 54-year drought with a Stanley Cup victory in 1994. The Cup visited Yankee Stadium for a baseball game and Belmont Park for the Belmont Stakes horse race. At one point, the Cup fell out of somebody's car. When it was returned to the Hockey Hall of Fame at the end of the summer, the Cup had been broken into four pieces. It took 36 hours of welding to repair it.

About the Author

By the age of 10, Eric Zweig was already a budding sports fanatic who was filling his school books with game reports instead of current events. He has been writing professionally about sports and sports history since graduating from Trent University in 1985. His articles have appeared in many Canadian publications including the *Toronto Star*, *The Globe and Mail*, the *Toronto Sun*, the *Ottawa Citizen*, the *Calgary Herald* and *The Beaver*. He has also been a writer/producer with CBC Radio Sports and TSN SportsRadio.

Eric is the author of many books, including *Hockey Night in the Dominion of Canada*, *The Big Book of Hockey for Kids*, *Super Scorers*, *Great Goalies*, *Dominant Defensemen*, and *Art Ross: The Hockey Legend Who Built the Bruins*. Eric also works with Dan Diamond and Associates on the annual *NHL Official Guide & Record Book*.

Eric is a member of the Society for International Hockey Research and the Society for American Baseball Research. He lives in Owen Sound, Ontario, with his wife Barbara, who is also a writer and editor. A former member of the Toronto Blue Jays grounds crew, he still has a champagne bottle from the club's first American League East Division title celebration in 1985.

Credits